BEER HIKING
BERLIN

THE TASTIEST WAY TO DISCOVER BERLIN

T0266941

Beer Hiking Berlin
The tastiest way to discover Berlin

Daniel Cole and Yvonne Hartmann

Photography: Daniel Cole, Yvonne Hartmann, Lisa Khanna
Typesetting and layout: Daniel Malak, Jędrzej Malak (maps)
Cover design: Ajša Zdravković
Editor: Ashley Curtis
Proofreader: Sonia Curtis

ISBN: 978-3-03964-010-2
First Edition: May 2023
Deposit copy in Switzerland: May 2023
Printed in the Czech Republic

© 2023 HELVETIQ (Helvetiq Sàrl)
Mittlere Straße 4
CH-4056 Basel

helvetiq.com

MIX
Paper from
responsible sources
FSC® C014138

BEER HIKING
BERLIN

THE TASTIEST WAY TO DISCOVER BERLIN

TABLE OF CONTENTS

1

INTRODUCTION

ABOUT THE AUTHORS

PHOTO © LISA KHANNA

Daniel Cole and Yvonne Hartmann are the creative team behind *Hiking and Drinking*, an online content platform documenting the world's best hikeable places for discovering regional wines, beers, and spirits. From offbeat vineyard trails to mountainous whiskey rambles, you can find it all on this unique storytelling hub for people who enjoy hiking and drinking.

Daniel was born in the UK, and his background lies primarily in music and travel journalism. A musician and obsessive record collector, he has bylines in various respected publications, including *Resident Advisor*, *Bandcamp Daily*, and *Drowned in Sound*. His love of music took him to festivals all over the world—providing the ideal opportunity to venture off the beaten path and discover new places. As his writing career took off, his journalism expanded into the travel sector, and it wasn't long before he was writing for *Thrillist*, *Discover Germany*, and *Lonely Planet*.

When Brexit was voted through, Daniel decided to make Berlin his permanent home. It wasn't a great leap, as he'd already been a German resident for over a decade. As a well-integrated expat and now officially a German citizen, it became his duty to ensure that he was fully familiar with one of the most important aspects of German life: beer. Although he was already a big fan, ensuring that he knew his Helles from his Weizen became not just a necessity, but a passion.

And so, Daniel started to combine his important research with his travels, dedicating his free time to visiting breweries throughout Germany. In Franconia, like many before him, he fell in love with the medieval town of Bamberg, and to this day the region's Keller, Dunkles, and unfiltered beers keep pulling him back. But Berlin's inimitable, rapidly evolving craft beer scene—with its iconic taprooms and countryside Brauhäuser—was right on his doorstep and ripe for exploration; writing a book about it all was the inevitable outcome.

Born and raised in Germany, Yvonne Hartmann also established herself in the music industry. She now works as an art director, brand expert, photographer, and lecturer. With many years of experience on the creative scene and a passion for visual storytelling, she supports artists and companies in developing authentic brands and campaigns, helping them gain public visibility with a professional look.

Yvonne inherited her love of nature, photography, and good wine from her grandfather, who was both an innkeeper and a gifted amateur photographer and hiker.

A travel enthusiast, Yvonne feels at home both in the mountains and on the beach. Having spent five years in Andalusia, Spain, she has developed a particular passion for southern European and Latin American countries. Wanderlust and curiosity have taken Yvonne around the world and throughout her home country—always with a camera on hand to collect and share her experiences with the wider world.

www.hiking-and-drinking.com
www.instagram.com/hiking_and_drinking
www.tiktok.com/@hikinganddrinking

ABOUT THIS BOOK

HIKING IN BERLIN

There's nothing better to remedy the soul and muscles after a long hike than a soothing glass of German beer. At the end of each walk listed in this book is a brewery or brewpub to help quench your thirst after your long expedition. What you are holding in your hands is a hiking guide to Berlin and beyond that takes you to some of the region's best spots for nature, history, and, of course, beer. Even if you live in Berlin, we hope that you'll discover new spots for hiking and new places to drink.

Berlin and its immediate surroundings feature a rich variety of landscapes, with expansive fields and farmland, broad woodlands, clear lakes, and of course a rich urban center that has been sculpted over time through the city's complex history.

That there is such a rich variety of natural landscapes in the region should come as no surprise. As the city grew over the centuries, its borders began to engulf the surrounding countryside and villages, taking in forests and large swathes of waterways. Thus, a walk in Berlin can take you along the Havel in the Grünewald forest, across the moorlands in Lübars, or along Berlin's old city wall path that runs through and around the center.

This book also includes select hikes on the outskirts of Berlin, including some that take you through the magnificent palatial grounds of Sanssouci, through the Barnim Forest to the north of the city, and around the orchards of Werder. All are easily accessible from Berlin's city center.

BEERS OF BERLIN

Before you jump the gun: Yes, German beer culture does exist outside of Bavaria! And in Berlin, it's thriving more now than ever before. Thanks to a burgeoning cosmopolitan community and some daring creativity and experimentation, Berlin's craft beer scene is diverse, expansive, and alive!

Looking back in time, Berlin has always had a strong relationship with beer and craft brewing. In the 19th century, the city was globally renowned for its Berliner Weiße, a light and sour beer that was often referred to as "the champagne of the north." During the 1900s, the city became a huge industrial player in beer production; Schultheiß and Berliner Kindl, for example, had several colossal factories located throughout the city. Their premises can still be seen on some of the walks described in this book.

Berlin was never going to be just a city that did mass-produced pilsners, however. Its position as a hub of independence and creativity saw to it that a new generation of brewers would bring new life and new ideas to the city's beer scene.

After the fall of the Berlin Wall, the city opened up to a whole range of new creative industries, attracting people from all across the world. The amount of available open space and low living costs allowed those with just a spark of an idea to live out their dreams, and it didn't take long before craft beer enthusiasts made their mark on the city.

Beer culture started to embody Berlin's independent spirit, with local brewers experimenting and adding new tastes for the urban community. And as the city saw a further influx of new residents from within and outside of Germany, the number of breweries and kinds of beer continued to increase. Brews now range from the traditional, wholesome beers produced by Hops & Barley to the assortment of full-flavored IPAs found in the tanks at Vagabund.

With so much on offer, Berlin is quickly becoming the beer capital of Germany—so much so that there are many breweries we couldn't include in this book. As a rule, we only included breweries that are open to the public and brewhouses with their own branded products. Among the many noteworthy beer manufacturers that we couldn't include in this book are some of our personal favorites: Gorilla Craft Beer, Motel, and, of course, the Berlin standard, Rollberg.

2

HOW IT WORKS

CHOOSE THE BEER OR THE HIKE

NAME OF THE HIKE ————→

REGION ————————

NAME OF THE BEER ————→

INFORMATION
ABOUT THE BEER ←————

INFORMATION
ABOUT THE HIKE ←————

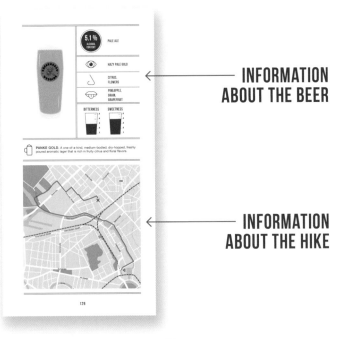

HOW TO USE THIS BOOK

To make these walks as accessible as possible, each hike starts at a train station and ends at a brewery or brewhouse. Each chapter describes the route in detail and notes highlights along the way.

The routes range from short (2 kilometers) to quite long (20 kilometers), with many of the shorter trails located within the city center. Should you feel adventurous, you can string some of these routes together to create something longer. For example, you can walk from Bräugier down Bernauer Straße to The Circus Hostel and then to Marcus Bräu and on to Liebhaftig.

Finding your way back after your beer-tasting adventures won't be challenging, as Berlin has an excellent transportation network. Public transport is easily reached from every one of the featured destinations.

We have largely used the German names for locations, including streets, bridges, towns, and lakes. Rather than call the Schlossbrücke the Castle Bridge, the Schloss Bridge, or the Schlossbrücke Bridge, for example, we simply call it the Schlossbrücke. To follow the directions in this book, it is therefore useful to know that Brücke means bridge; Straße, Weg, Chaussee, and Allee all mean street (of one kind or another); Platz means square or piazza; and See means lake. This allows us to use the names you will see on signs and maps, without the language becoming too cumbersome.

TRAIL AND BEER RATINGS

The ratings and scales in this book are entirely subjective, as they must be. Since this book predominantly features city hikes, it's a bit different from books about mountains or other wild terrain.

Fun fact: Berlin is very, very flat. Thus, the hiking difficulty scale is largely based on the route's length and the time it will take you to complete it.

The flavor ratings within these pages are based on our own extensive knowledge of beer. Where you come from in the world might affect your expectations of how these beers should taste. We've tried to be as objective as possible, but of course you are welcome to disagree!

BEFORE SETTING OFF

CHECK YOUR GEAR

EQUIPMENT/CLOTHING

The hiking areas covered in this book alternate between urban and rural landscapes, so it's important to consider this as you prepare. If you're hiking in the city, you won't be too far away from shelter should it rain, or from a convenience store if you run out of water. As Berlin's weather varies greatly throughout the year, it should also influence how you prepare. Here is a list of the equipment we recommend always bringing with you:

- Bring this hiking guide with you to ensure you always find the way.

- Bring a smart phone and/or a city map.

- If you're hiking outside the city in Zone C, and in some Zone B areas, then you'll need to be prepared for outdoor environments. When hiking through forests, it's important to wear sturdy boots and bring plenty of water and bug spray.

- If hiking in the spring and summer months, dress appropriately and bring sunscreen, a hat, and sunglasses.

- In the autumn and winter months, wear thermals when needed with plenty of additional layers, a hat, and footwear that can withstand rain, snow, and ice.

- There are a lot of bathing spots along the walks, so when noted, bring a towel and something to change into (or not—it's Germany after all!).

- Berlin is prone to lots of precipitation, so whatever the season, bring rainproof gear and make sure your day bag is protected.

- Make sure you bring plenty of water, snacks, and, of course, your camera to capture special moments.

- If you're traveling with public transportation, you'll need a ticket.

- Many establishments in Berlin are still reluctant to accept card payments, so bring enough cash with you.

WEATHER

Berlin's weather features extremes on both ends of the spectrum. Temperatures in the summer months average in the high twenties Celsius but can run as high as the mid-thirties. Winters can be extremely cold, dropping into freezing temperatures, with extremes reaching to negative ten Celsius and even below. You can also expect a lot of snow and ice in the first few months of the year, along with harsh winds. And whatever time of year, there's always plenty of precipitation.

GETTING AROUND

Each hike described in this book is easily accessible, with a starting point located at one of the city's many public railway stations. All of the trailheads are located in the city's ABC zone. This means that even though some of the trailheads and breweries are located outside of the city, such as those in Potsdam and Bernau, you can still reach them using a normal ABC ticket.

Tickets can be purchased online or using an app, which we highly recommend. AB tickets are required for inner-city journeys, while C-zone tickets are required for journeys into Brandenburg. Always check the city map to make sure you know which ticket to get.

Tickets can be bought on buses and trams, but you'll be required to pay in cash, so make sure you bring some with you. Always make sure to check bus and train timetables before leaving on your journey.

UNDERSTANDING STREET SIGNS

On your journeys through the city, you'll see a multitude of differently colored signs designed to help you find your way around.

The majority of these will be small numbered blue rectangles on a white background. These refer to specific long-distance hikes within the Berlin zone and are referenced where appropriate in the following chapters.

There are also larger white signs with green text. These mark designated national bike routes, which are also referenced throughout the book.

ONLINE RESOURCES

Public transport website: www.bvg.de
Berlin news and updates: www.berlin.de
Berlin tourist info: www.visitberlin.de

3

MAP & INDEX

MAP

96

ORANIENBURG

10

111

HENNIGSDORF

28

27

29

2

5

1

35

10

39

115

POTSDAM

37

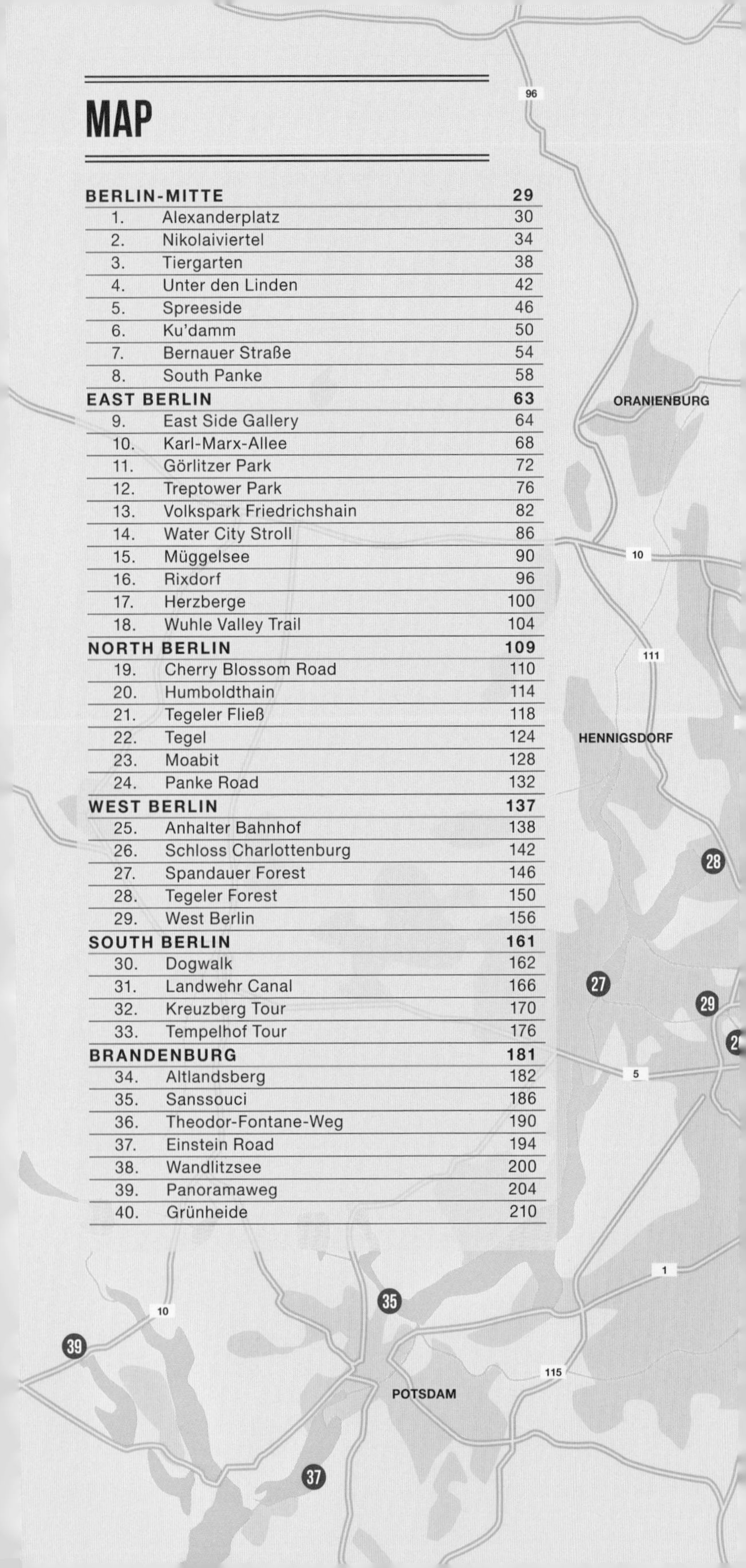

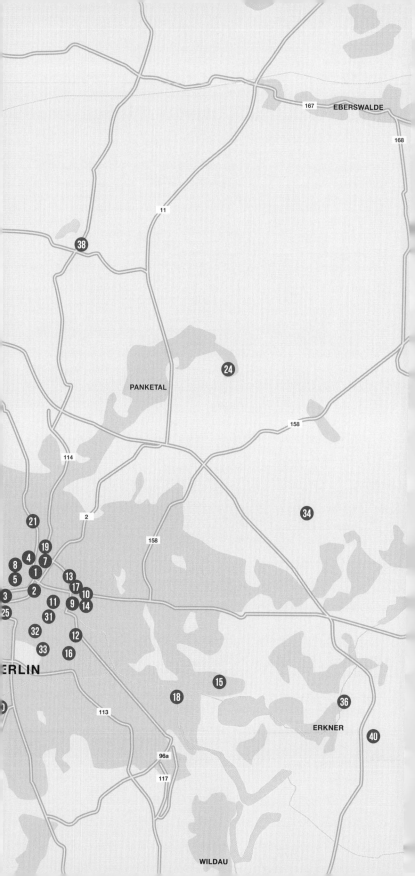

INDEX OF HIKES

NAME OF THE ROUTE	STARTING POINT	LENGTH	MAP
Alexanderplatz	Spittelmarkt U-Bahn	4.5 Km	1
Altlandsberg	Neuenhagen S-Bahn	8.5 Km	34
Anhalter Bahnhof	Hausvogteiplatz U-Bahn	5 Km	25
Bernauer Straße	Eberswalder Straße U-Bahn	5 Km	7
Cherry Blossom Road	Schönholz S-Bahn	7.7 Km	19
Dogwalk	Südkreuz S-Bahn	9 Km	30
East Side Gallery	Ostbahnhof	2.5 Km	9
Einstein Road	Potsdam Hauptbahnhof	13.5 Km	37
Görlitzer Park	Treptower Park S-Bahn	3.3 Km	11
Grünheide	Erkner S-Bahn	10.4 Km (One Way)	40
Herzberge	Friedrichsfelde-Ost S-Bahn	12 Km	17
Humboldthain	Voltastraße U-Bahn	4.7 Km	20
Karl-Marx-Allee	Schillingstraße U-Bahn	3.5 Km	10
Kreuzberg Tour	Platz der Luftbrücke U-Bahn	5 Km	32
Ku'damm	Wittenbergplatz U-Bahn	3.4 Km	6
Landwehr Canal	Hallesches Tor U-Bahn	4.9 Km	31
Moabit	Hauptbahnhof	7 Km	23
Müggelsee	Friedrichshagen S-Bahn	18.3 Km	15
Nikolaiviertel	Museumsinsel U-Bahn	2.1 Km	2
Panke Road	Buch S-Bahn	14 Km (One Way)	24
Panoramaweg	Werder (Havel) Station	15 Km (One Way)	39
Rixdorf	Hermannplatz U-Bahn	5 Km	16
Sanssouci	Bahnhof Potsdam Park Sanssouci	7.8 Km	35
Schloss Charlottenburg	Jungfernheide U-Bahn	4.5 Km	26
South Panke	Wedding S-Bahn	5.7 Km	8
Spandauer Forest	Hennigsdorf S-Bahn	15 Km	27
Spreeside	Bellevue S-Bahn	6.6 Km	5
Tegel	Halemweg U-Bahn	9.2 Km	22
Tegeler Fließ	Waidmannslust S-Bahn	16 Km	21
Tegeler Forest	Heiligensee S-Bahn	13.7 Km	28
Tempelhof Tour	Südstern U-Bahn	3.2 Km	33
Theodor-Fontane-Weg	Erkner S-Bahn	10 Km	36
Tiergarten	Zoologischer Garten S-Bahn	4.2 Km	3
Treptower Park	Treptower Park S-Bahn	7.5 Km	12
Unter den Linden	Brandenburger Tor S-Bahn	4.3 Km	4
Volkspark Friedrichshain	Senefelderplatz U-Bahn	7 Km	13
Wandlitzsee	Bahnhof Wandlitzsee	10 Km	38
Water City Stroll	Treptower Park S-Bahn	6.3 Km	14
West Berlin	Grunewald S-Bahn	11.5 Km	29
Wuhle Valley Trail	Ahrensfelde S-Bahn	19 Km	18

BREWERIES & BEERS

BREWERY	BEER	PAGE
Berliner Marcus Bräu	Marcus Bräu Pils	30
SBB Altlandsberg	Altlandsberger Kupfer	182
BRLO BRWHOUSE	BRLO Pale Ale	138
Leibhaftig	Dunkel	54
Bräugier Brewpub	Summer IPA	110
BrewDog DogTap	Elvis Juice	162
Privatbrauerei Schalander	Schalander Pils	64
Forsthaus Templin	Potsdamer Stange	194
Heidenpeters	Pale Ale	72
Flügel's Hof	Flügelbräu Dunkel	210
Protokoll	Research Chemicals	100
Vagabund Brauerei Kesselhaus	Day Party	114
Hops & Barley	Friedrichshainer Pilsner	68
Brauhaus Südstern	Orang Utan Ale	170
Vaust	Vaust Dunkel	50
Schoppe Bräu Taproom im BKK	Sommermärchen	166
Eschenbräu	Panke Gold	128
Brau- & Genusswerkstatt Berlin-Friedrichshagen	Dolle Molle Kupfersamt	90
Brauhaus Georgbräu	Georgbräu Hell	34
Erste Bernauer Braugenossenschaft	Das Bernauer	132
Zum Rittmeister	Rittmeisters Schwarzbier	204
Rotbart	Rotbart Rotbier	96
Meierei im Neuen Garten	Meierei Rotbier	186
Lemke Am Schloss	Lemke Weizen	142
The Castle	Berliner Hopscor Pale Ale	58
Brauhaus Spandau	Spandauer Havelbräu	146
Unverhopft Taproom	Unverhopft Raw	46
Schneeeule Salon für Berliner Bierkultur	Marlene	124
Two Fellas Brewery	California Common	118
Kubi's Point	Messing	150
Brauhaus Neulich	Neulich Original	176
Woltersdorfer Schleusenbrauerei	Woltersdorfer Dunkel	190
Lindenbräu am Potsdamer Platz	Hopfinger Berlin	38
Berliner Berg Brauerei	Berliner Weiße	76
The Circus Hostel Microbrewery	Amber Lager	42
Brauerei Flessa	Mandarina	82
Brauhaus Wandlitz	Wandlitzer Dunkel	200
Straßenbräu Taproom	Stralauer Pils	86
Fuerst Wiacek	After Party	156
Schlossplatzbrauerei Köpenick	Helles	104

4

THE BEER HIKES

BERLIN-MITTE

ALEXANDERPLATZ

BERLIN'S OLD HEART

MITTE, BERLIN

▷⋯ STARTING POINT	⋯✗ DESTINATION
SPITTELMARKT U-BAHN STATION	**BERLINER MARCUS BRÄU**
🍺 BEER NAME	🔀 DIFFICULTY
MARCUS BRÄU PILS	**EASY**
🚃 TRANSPORT	🕐 DURATION
U2	**45 MIN.**
🏔 ZONE	↦ LENGTH
A	**4.5 KM**
🔍 HIGHLIGHTS	〰 ELEVATION GAIN
KÖLLNISCHER PARK, PAROCHIAL KIRCHE, WELTZEITUHR	ASCENT: 10 M DESCENT: 10 M

4.9 % ALCOHOL CONTENT	PILSNER
(eye)	CLOUDY, LEMON-YELLOW
(nose)	SWEET, FLOWERY, HOPS
(mouth)	HONEY, SPICE, MALTY

BITTERNESS   SWEETNESS

 MARCUS BRÄU PILS. Far from your classic pils, this fresh, hazy, and lightly carbonated beer features an exciting combination of tastes that will leave you pleasantly surprised and very refreshed.

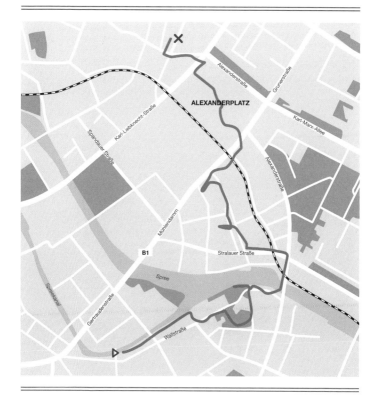

HIKE DESCRIPTION

The area along Märkisches Ufer is one of Berlin's oldest districts. Walking along the banks of Fischerinsel, which once made up the center of Cölln—the former city twinned with Old Berlin—you'll see remnants of long-gone times, including old passenger boats, restaurants, and townhouses. It's befitting, then, that this walk finishes at a restaurant that feels out of time in a city that is growing up too fast—a place where you can still enjoy traditional meals and the feeling of the Berlin of yore.

From the station, head east along the unnamed waterfront footpath, taking in the collection of antique sailing vessels moored in the historic harbor. After 500 meters, at the Inselbrücke, take a right on Inselstraße and then head east on Wallstraße to check out Köllnischer Park. Here you'll find, in addition to the Märkisches Museum (which exhibits remnants of Berlin's past), a bear pit that housed real-life bears (which are on the city's emblem) until 2015.

Continue on Wallstraße, which becomes Märkisches Ufer. Turn left and cross the river on Jannowitzbrücke. Be sure to check out the boats lining up to pass through the Mühlendamm lock. Take a left on Stralauer Straße and then, after 250 meters, a right on Waisenstraße. As you head north, you'll see some of the only surviving remnants of the centuries-old city wall that once marked Berlin's boundary. After 150 meters, you'll reach the 300-year-old Parochial Church on your left.

The "checking off all of Berlin's old things" doesn't stop here! On your right is Berlin's oldest restaurant, Zur Letzten Instanz, which dates to 1621. It's a fine establishment with incredible traditional dishes; make sure you visit this restaurant before leaving Berlin.

After Zur Letzten Instanz, turn right onto Littenstraße and head north until the junction with Grunerstraße. Turn right and cross Grunerstraße

at the pedestrian crossing. Pass directly across the bustling Alexander-platz, perhaps gazing up at the iconic TV Tower (Fernsehturm).

Walk northwest past the Weltzeituhr, cross the tram lines, and, after 350 meters, turn right on Karl-Liebknecht-Straße. After 100 meters, at the traffic lights, head west on Memhardstraße. You'll soon see the craft beer sign outside Marcus Bräu at the corner of Münzstraße and Rosa-Luxemburg-Straße.

BERLINER MARCUS BRÄU

The Marcus Brewery is an island of tradition in a sea of gentrified store-fronts and multinational brands. As the city center becomes ever more commodified with international outlets, this old-school restaurant retains its classic, authentic German atmosphere. As you enter the inconspicu-ous-looking, moderately sized establishment, you'll see brewing tanks behind the bar and classic ornamental beer steins lined up above the dining tables. Food-wise, you'll be hard pressed to find fine German classics such as schnitzel and pork knuckle at a better price in this part of town. The beer is also as fresh as it comes, with a Pilsner and either a Dunkel or a Rotbier served up by the liter for thirsty drinkers.

ADDRESS

Berliner Marcus Bräu
Münzstraße 1–3
10178 Berlin
+49 30 2476985
www.volkskochtopf.de

Photos © Daniel Cole

NIKOLAIVIERTEL

BERLIN'S OLD CITY QUARTER

MITTE, BERLIN

▷··· STARTING POINT	···✗ DESTINATION
MUSEUMSINSEL U-BAHN STATION	**BRAUHAUS GEORGBRÄU**
🍺 BEER NAME	DIFFICULTY
GEORGBRÄU HELL	**EASY**
🚆 TRANSPORT	🕐 DURATION
U5	**30 MIN.**
⛰ ZONE	↦ LENGTH
A	**2.1 KM**
🔍 HIGHLIGHTS	〰 ELEVATION GAIN
JUNGFERN BRIDGE, ST. NICOLAS' CHURCH, KNOBLAUCHHAUS, ST. GEORGE STATUE	ASCENT: 10 M DESCENT: 10 M

5.0 % ALCOHOL CONTENT

HELLES

AMBER WITH WHITE
CREAMY HEAD

MALTY,
HERBY

HERBY,
DRIED FRUIT,
CARAMEL

BITTERNESS

SWEETNESS

 GEORGBRÄU HELL. A medium-bodied bitter and malty Helles that
typifies Berlin beer.

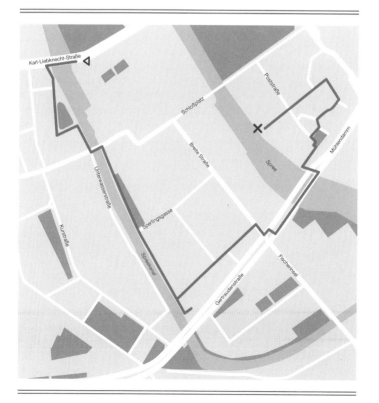

HIKE DESCRIPTION

In the heart of Berlin's bustling urban sprawl, a tiny piece of history is hidden away behind some unremarkable facades. Next to the city's town hall, you'll find a remnant of a long-ago time. Dating back to the 1200s, the Nikolaiviertel is the oldest part of the city, full of cobbled roads, quaint cafés, restaurants, and a magnificent cathedral. Although most of it was rebuilt after the war, it still retains the charm and character of a medieval outpost.

Leaving Museumsinsel, head west on Unter den Linden, cross the Schlossbrücke, and then head immediately south following the canal on Schinkelplatz. At Werderscher Markt, head east and cross the Schleusenbrücke. Turn right immediately on Friedrichsgracht and follow it for 400 meters. Along this walkway, you'll pass an old Soviet mosaic by Walter Womacka. Soon you'll reach the Jungfernbrücke, the oldest surviving bridge in Berlin.

At the end of Friedrichsgracht you'll be greeted by the statue of Saint Gertrude, the patron saint of travelers and pilgrims. Turn left and follow Kleine Getraudenstraße for 700 meters, cross the Spree, and arrive outside Ephraim-Palais, which dates back to the 18th century. Follow the steps immediately in front of the Palais down into the old city quarter, staying left and then going counterclockwise around Nikolaikirche, the oldest church in Berlin, before passing Zum Nußbaum, one of the oldest bars in Berlin. Seeing a theme here?

Here in the old town, you'll find classical- and baroque-style buildings, museums, and statues of legendary characters from Berlin's history. The most noteworthy landmark is the Knoblauchhaus (named after the wealthy, merchant Knoblauch family), one of the most pristinely preserved buildings in the city. As you circle around the church, head directly west onto Propststraße to the statue of St. George and the Dragon near the river; here you'll find the Georgbräu.

BRAUHAUS GEORGBRÄU

Georgbräu is a traditional large German restaurant with an abundance of riverside seating during the summer months. Inside, it features long wooden tables and copper pipes running across the bar that pump the freshly brewed beers into the taps. The food consists of classic German dishes such as schnitzel, pork-knuckle, and herring. The vibe and atmosphere befit the classical quarter, and the restaurant offers impeccable service to boot. The brewery serves up Helles, Dunkel, and Bockbiers all year round; you can often see them being freshly brewed as you pass through the main doors.

ADDRESS

Brauhaus Georgbräu
Spreeufer 4
10178 Berlin
+49 30 2424244
www.georgbraeu.de

Photos © Yvonne Hartmann

TIERGARTEN

A GREEN OASIS CONNECTING ALL OF BERLIN'S CENTRAL LANDMARKS

MITTE, BERLIN

▷⋯ STARTING POINT	⋯✕ DESTINATION
ZOOLOGISCHER GARTEN S-BAHN STATION	**LINDENBRÄU AM POTSDAMER PLATZ**
🍺 BEER NAME	🀫 DIFFICULTY
HOPFINGER BERLIN	**EASY**
🚃 TRANSPORT	🕐 DURATION
U2, U3, U9	**1 H**
🏔 ZONE	↦ LENGTH
A	**4.2 KM**
🔍 HIGHLIGHTS	〰 ELEVATION GAIN
ZOOLOGISCHER GARTEN, TIERGARTEN, NEUER SEE, SONY CENTER	ASCENT: 10 M DESCENT: 10 M

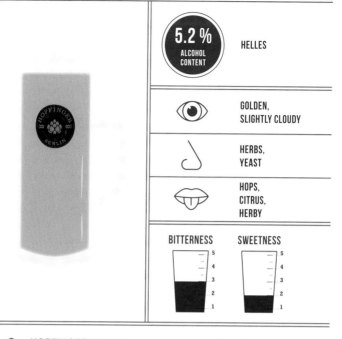

5.2 % ALCOHOL CONTENT	HELLES
👁	GOLDEN, SLIGHTLY CLOUDY
👃	HERBS, YEAST
👄	HOPS, CITRUS, HERBY

BITTERNESS	SWEETNESS
5 4 3 2 1	5 4 3 2 1

HOPFINGER BERLIN. Subtly aromatic and bitter, this full-bodied Helles delights with herbal notes and tastes of wheat and lemon on the tongue.

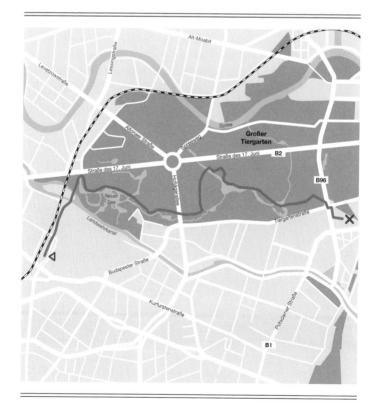

HIKE DESCRIPTION

 A green oasis located in the city center, the Tiergarten is a sanctuary from the ongoing ruckus that engulfs Berlin. The former hunting grounds literally provide a breath of fresh air. The gardens, fields, and natural waterways stretch all the way from the Zoologischer Garten to the Brandenburg Gate. The park is flanked on either side by some of Berlin's most important landmarks and includes some of the city's most prized natural wonders. The walk itself may only take a couple of hours, but one could easily spend an entire afternoon daydreaming in this sanctuary of natural delights.

Leaving the station on the side of the zoo, turn left and head north. Cross Hertzallee and continue on the footpath. Pass the zoo to your right and, after 350 meters, cross the canal at Schleusenkrug, a beautiful beer garden looking out across the water. Still heading north, take note of the antiquated gas streetlights on your left, which have been preserved for over a century.

Upon reaching Straße des 17. Juni, turn right and then immediately right again and follow the waterside path on Großer Weg south into Tiergarten, as it curves along Neuer See. As you watch the tourists in the rowboats flitting about on the open water, carry on walking for another kilometer until you reach Hofjägerallee.

Cross Hofjägerallee and take note of the iconic Siegessäule (victory column) on your left. After the crossing, follow Großer Weg back under the trees and turn left and follow the path for 400 meters. After crossing Tiergartengewässer, turn right and then left into the Rose Garden, one of the park's most colorful and emblematic sites. After you've smelled the roses, leave the garden at its southern exit and head east. Follow the waterside path for 500 meters, turn right, and cross the bridge that takes you to Luiseninsel.

Curve left around the gardens and then turn left on Ahornsteig and follow it for 400 meters. At Bellevueallee, turn right and proceed for 200 meters. At the junction of Tiergartenstraße and Ben-Gurion-Straße, head south, taking note of the elegant Philharmonie as you pass it by.

After a few hundred meters, take a left and enter the Sony Center, a modernistic commercial hub with some impressive lighting rigs and roof fittings—and, of course, Lindenbräu.

LINDENBRÄU AM POTSDAMER PLATZ

If you're longing for cozy ambience and Bavarian charm, look no further than the centrally located Lindenbräu am Potsdamer Platz. The interior is styled like an alpine inn, with all the requisite wooden fittings. The beer lobby just inside the entrance is centered around the brewery's former copper kettles, relics from when the brewing used to happen on-site. In the restaurant, you can feast on mouthwatering traditionally cooked German and Austrian dishes. The beer to wash down these hearty meals is as good as you would expect of such a place: Hopfinger Berlin, Zwickel, and traditional Weizen beers are on tap all year round.

ADDRESS

Lindenbräu am Potsdamer Platz
Bellevuestraße 3–5
10785 Berlin
+49 30 25751280
restaurant@lindenbraeu-berlin.de
www.bier-genuss.berlin

Photos © Yvonne Hartmann

UNTER DEN LINDEN

THE BEST BEER TOUR IN CENTRAL BERLIN

MITTE, BERLIN

▷··· STARTING POINT	···✕ DESTINATION
BRANDENBURGER TOR S-BAHN STATION	**THE CIRCUS HOSTEL MICROBREWERY**
🍺 BEER NAME	DIFFICULTY
AMBER LAGER	**EASY**
🚃 TRANSPORT	🕐 DURATION
S1, S2, S25, S25, U5	**1 H 15 MIN.**
⛰ ZONE	↦ LENGTH
A	**4.3 KM**
🔍 HIGHLIGHTS	〰 ELEVATION GAIN
BRANDENBURGER GATE, HUMBOLDT UNIVERSITY, ALTE NATIONALGALERIE	ASCENT: 10 M DESCENT: 0 M

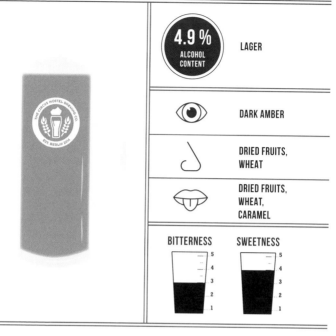

4.9 % ALCOHOL CONTENT	LAGER
	DARK AMBER
	DRIED FRUITS, WHEAT
	DRIED FRUITS, WHEAT, CARAMEL

BITTERNESS   SWEETNESS

 AMBER LAGER. This sweet-caramel, medium-bodied malty lager stands out with its fruity aroma and smooth, rich texture.

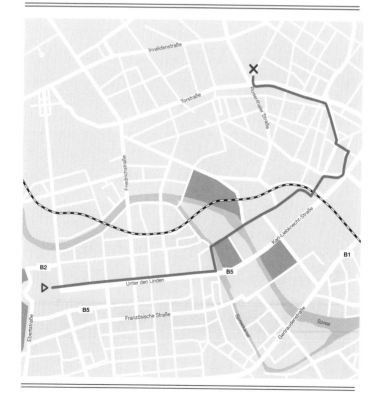

HIKE DESCRIPTION

There is no location more recognizable than the Brandenburger Tor in Berlin. This national landmark symbolizing the reunification of Germany is located between Tiergarten and the sprawling boulevard of Unter den Linden, which stretches all the way from the Brandenburger Tor to Museumsinsel. Along it you can find some of the city's best-known landmarks, including the Humboldt Forum and the Staatsoper (opera house). The road dates back to the 16th century; with its many museums and monuments, it's the very epitome of classical Berlin. This walk also takes you to the city center's best breweries and tap houses.

Starting at Brandenburger Tor, head east on Unter den Linden for a kilometer. Before crossing the Kupfergraben onto Museumsinsel and just after passing the German Historical Museum, turn left and follow the canal to the north. Cross the Eiserne Brücke in front of the James Simon Gallery, head east beneath the colonnade in front of the Alte Nationalgalerie, and cross the romantic Friedrichsbrücke, taking in the view of the Berliner Dom.

Head east for 500 meters along Anna-Louisa-Karsch-Straße, which turns into Rochstraße. Turn right on the footpath just before the overhead rail tracks. After 100 meters, this small detour ends at the Lemke Biermeisterei, worthy of a quick drink before you carry on.

From the Lemke Biermeisterei, cross Dirckenstraße and head north on Rosa-Luxemburg-Straße. Head east on Memhardstraße for a few hundred meters. This will land you at BraufactuM am Alexanderplatz, another popular taproom.

From BraufactuM, head north on Karl-Liebknecht-Straße for 200 meters, passing the Hofbräu Wirtshaus on your right. Head west on Hirtenstraße for 300 meters and then turn right on Almstadtstraße. Head north on Almstadtstraße for 300 meters and then turn left on Rosa-Luxemburg-

Straße. Just before you hit Torstraße, you'll see the Kaschk Bar by BRLO on your left.

Continue westward on Torstraße for 600 meters, eventually passing Mikkeller Berlin, and arrive at the junction with Brunnenstraße and Weinbergsweg. Head northeast on Weinbergsweg and you'll soon see The Circus Hostel Brewery on your right, with the bar snuggly located underground.

THE CIRCUS HOSTEL MICROBREWERY

Don't fret—this is far from your average hostel bar. Discretely located beneath one of the city's biggest hostels is a cozy and finely styled cellar bar, complete with an excellent cocktail menu, a library full of beer and city guides, and a microbrewery on full display. The dimly lit, centrally located bar makes up for its size with its buzzing atmosphere. Regular events include ever-popular karaoke sessions. With a buzzing streetside café above serving the punters by day, during the evening the bar's taps offer local guest beers in addition to regularly rotating house brews, with Bocks served up at special times of the year.

ADDRESS

The Circus Hostel
Weinbergsweg 1a
10119 Berlin
+49 30 20003939
info@circus-berlin.de
www.circus-berlin.de

Photos © Yvonne Hartmann

SPREESIDE

A ROMANTIC WALK ALONG THE CITY'S RIVER

MITTE, BERLIN

▷⋯ STARTING POINT	⋯✕ DESTINATION
BELLEVUE S-BAHN STATION	**UNVERHOPFT TAPROOM**
🍺 BEER NAME	🎲 DIFFICULTY
UNVERHOPFT RAW	**EASY**
🚆 TRANSPORT	⏲ DURATION
S3, S5, S7, S9	**1.5 H**
⛰ ZONE	⊢→ LENGTH
A	**6.6 KM**
🔍 HIGHLIGHTS	〰 ELEVATION GAIN
HAUS DER KULTUREN DER WELT, REICHSTAG, PERGAMON MUSEUM	ASCENT: 10 M DESCENT: 10 M

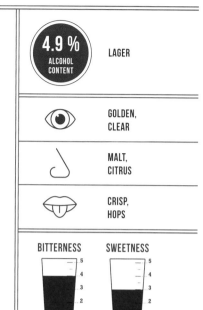

4.9 % ALCOHOL CONTENT	LAGER
(eye)	GOLDEN, CLEAR
(nose)	MALT, CITRUS
(mouth)	CRISP, HOPS

BITTERNESS

5
4
3
2
1

SWEETNESS

5
4
3
2
1

UNVERHOPFT RAW. The crisp and clean complexion of this modern lager, as well as its rich hoppy character, make for a staggeringly refreshing experience accented by highly palatable subtle notes of fruit.

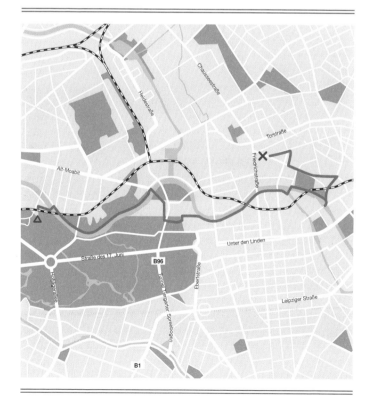

HIKE DESCRIPTION

The Spree embankment in Berlin's city center is akin to Germany's very own riviera. Here, beer gardens and elegant promenades line up side-by-side with governmental buildings and lush green waterfront parks. Busking classical musicians play along the riverfront, while dancers tango in front of the Romanesque Bode Museum. The capital's historic landmarks line the water, and Baroque and Modernist architecture form an interesting tapestry of urban planning.

Leaving the station on the Spree side, head east and cross Gericke-steg, a classically designed, 100-year-old footbridge that provides stunning views of the Moabit district. Then head immediately southeast on Helgoländer Ufer. After 100 meters, the road turns into a footpath that runs along the river, passing the backside of the Bellevue Palace on the other side of the river.

After 500 meters, the path crosses the Lutherbrücke, carrying on between lush green embankments and heading toward the Memorial to the First German Homosexual Emancipation Movement. On the other side of the river, the modernist Haus der Kulturen der Welt faces out onto the water, just a few hundred meters away from the German Chancellery.

After 400 meters, head south across the Moltkebrücke. Then head down Willy-Brandt-Straße for 250 meters into the government district. Head south for 120 meters on the grassy pathway that passes the parliament buildings and embassies and then turn to the left and take Paul-Löbe-Allee back to the waterfront, passing the Reichstag on your right. Carry on eastward along the Spree for 1.2 kilometers, pass beneath the Spreebrücke and the Friedrichstraße station, and continue on Am Kupfergraben toward Monbijoubrücke, crossing the Spree over the pedestrian bridge to the Bode Museum.

Directly after the bridge and just before the outdoor Monbijou Theater, turn right and follow the river again, passing the dancefloor where, on a warm summer's evening, partners can be seen dancing the tango as the sun sets over the water. Six hundred meters onward at Friedrichsbrücke, which looks out toward the Berliner Dom, turn left and head north on Burgstraße, passing beneath Hackescher Markt station and through a promenade full of street vendors and restaurants. At Oranienburger Straße, head west for one kilometer, past Monbijou Park on your left and the New Synagogue on your right. Turn to the right on Auguststraße and find Bar Amélie on the right-hand side.

UNVERHOPFT TAPROOM

The Unverhopft Taproom is located inside Bar Amélie, an upscale and sophisticated cocktail and craft beer bar in Berlin's central district. Intimate and cozy, the bar offers modern cocktails while the taps offer a selection of in-house brewed beers as well as guest offerings. It's a truly unique and swanky place to flex your palate on some modern beers. The Unverhopft team is never shy about embracing change, constantly introducing new limited-range beers. Along with their permanent range of Pilsners, you can find mate-infused brews, fruity IPAs, stouts, and more.

ADDRESS

Unverhopft Taproom
Bar Amélie
Auguststraße 2
10117 Berlin
+49 177 7169445
mail@unverhopft.com
www.unverhopft.com

Photos © Daniel Cole

KU'DAMM

HIGH STREET GOODS AND TOP VEGAN FOOD

CHARLOTTENBURG, BERLIN

▷··· STARTING POINT	···✗ DESTINATION
WITTENBERGPLATZ U-BAHNSTATION	**VAUST**
🍺 BEER NAME	🔢 DIFFICULTY
VAUST DUNKEL	**EASY**
🚃 TRANSPORT	🕐 DURATION
U1, U2, U3	**45 MIN.**
⛰ ZONE	↦ LENGTH
A	**3.4 KM**
🔍 HIGHLIGHTS	〰 ELEVATION GAIN
KADEWE, KAISER WILHELM MEMORIAL CHURCH, KANTSTRASSE	ASCENT: 0 M DESCENT: 0 M

4.9% ALCOHOL CONTENT	DUNKLES
(eye)	CLOUDY DARK CHOCOLATEY BROWN
(nose)	MALTY, CHOCOLATE, CARAMEL
(mouth)	BITTER CHOCOLATE, MALT

BITTERNESS	SWEETNESS
5 4 3 2 1	5 4 3 2 1

VAUST DUNKEL. A refreshing malty and sweet dark beer with a caramel and chocolate aroma and a subtly bitter flavor that doesn't overwhelm the palate.

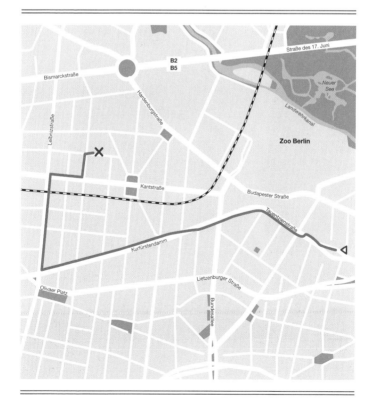

HIKE DESCRIPTION

On the opulent and chic Kurfürstendamm shopping boulevard in West Berlin, you'll find high-street outlets and European street-side dining. Home to shops from some of the world's biggest and most opulent brands, the street—known as Ku'Damm to the locals—is a center of glitz and luxury. Along this "Shopping Straße," you'll pass the KaDeWe center, Berlin's very own Bloom-ingdale's. You'll also find the partly destroyed Kaiser Wilhelm Memorial Church, one of the city's most iconic landmarks. From West Berlin luxury, our route heads through the city's finest food district to a delightful modern vegan restaurant with its own homemade beers.

Leave the impressive Art Nouveau–style Wittenbergplatz station on Tauentzienstraße and head northwest, taking time to observe the KaDeWe shopping extravaganza on your left. If time permits, visit the food court on the top floor (which includes a BRLO bar) and sample some of the finest delicacies in the city. As the road proceeds, it passes beneath a giant iron-chain statue symbolizing the city's reunification and then runs by the Kaiser Wilhelm Memorial Church on the right.

Amidst the series of shopping centers on the road is the Europa Center, one of Berlin's oldest malls, in front of which the city's prominent Christmas market is held in December.

From Kaiser Wilhelm Memorial Church, proceed for 1.6 kilometers and then turn right on Leibnizstraße. Stop for a few selfies on the Walter-Benjamin-Platz, a modern plaza with multicolored umbrellas hanging between the stores.

After 600 meters, take a right on Kantstraße, one of the best streets for Chinese and Taiwanese restaurants in Berlin. Continue on Kantstraße for 250 meters; just before Savignyplatz, head north on Schülterstraße for a block. Then, take a quick right into the sleepy and quiet Pestalozzistraße, where you'll find the Vaust restaurant tables set up on the left side of the street.

VAUST

One of Berlin's best homemade beers can be found in a modern and cozy vegan restaurant located in the city's western district. Offering mouthwatering vegan alternatives to traditional dishes such as ceviche, schnitzel, and currywurst, and with new and creative avant-garde dishes on the menu as well, Vaust is one of the most popular meat-free diners in town. The in-house beer offerings are produced by talented local brewmaster Wolfgang Grabolle using the Brewbaker facilities in Reinickendorf. The in-house Pilsner and Dunkel beers are available all year round, as are some mixed varieties including a mango-chili beer made with a sweet homemade syrup.

ADDRESS

Vaust Braugaststätte
Pestalozzistraße 8
10625 Berlin
+49 30 54599160
info@vaust.berlin
www.vaust.berlin

Photos © Yvonne Hartmann

BERNAUER STRASSE

A PEACEFUL STRETCH THROUGH A ONCE DIVIDED NEIGHBORHOOD

PRENZLAUER BERG, BERLIN

▷⋯ STARTING POINT	⋯✗ DESTINATION
EBERSWALDER STRASSE U-BAHN STATION	**LEIBHAFTIG**
🍺 BEER NAME	🎛 DIFFICULTY
DUNKEL	**EASY**
🚋 TRANSPORT	🕐 DURATION
U2	**1 H 15 MIN.**
⛰ ZONE	↦ LENGTH
B	**5 KM**
🔎 HIGHLIGHTS	〰 ELEVATION GAIN
CONRAD SCHUMANN MEMORIAL, BERLIN WALL MEMORIAL, ZION CHURCH, PFEFFERBERG	ASCENT: 20 M DESCENT: 20 M

	5.1 % ALCOHOL CONTENT	DUNKLES
	(eye)	DARK MAHOGANY AND A CREAMY WHITE HEAD
	(nose)	SLIGHT ROASTED MALT
	(mouth)	DARK FRUITS, ROASTED MALT, BREAD

BITTERNESS	SWEETNESS
5 4 3 2 1	5 4 3 2 1

DUNKEL. With Franken qualities, this light and sweet dark beer gains complexity after a few sips as subtle chocolate and earthy flavors mingle with its roasted malt essence.

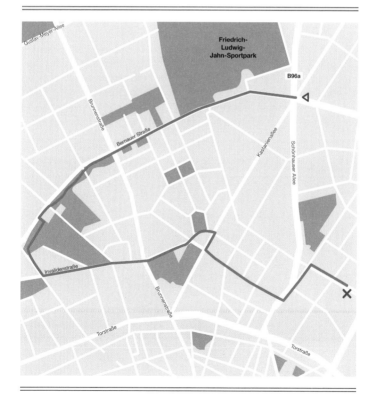

HIKE DESCRIPTION

Between 1961 and 1989, many people tried to escape the confines of the East at the Berlin Wall crossing at Bernauer Straße. Today, the street bears witness to this notorious border crossing: it's lined with artworks, monuments, and a museum. It's one of the most important segments of the Berlin Wall, featuring a walk that passes along the former death strip and back into the city center, now filled with chic modern restaurants and boutique bars.

From the station, head west on Eberswalder Straße, which turns into Bernauer Straße, passing the lively Mauerpark on your right. After 1.2 kilometers, reach the corner of Brunnenstraße. On the side of the building is a looming memorial to Conrad Schumann, the soldier immortalized in a legendary image that shows him jumping across the barbed wire that separated East and West Berlin.

Further down Bernauer Straße, alongside other memorials and artworks, lie peaceful gardens filled with barley, vegetables, and wildflowers. Follow the remaining segment of the Wall and pass tributes to those who died on Bernauer Straße. After a kilometer, turn left on Gartenstraße and then east on Invalidenstraße. You'll pass Mitte's BrewDog restaurant before crossing Brunnen Straße once again and heading up Veteranen Straße.

At the genial neighborhood at the top of the street is the 19th-century Zion Church, a beautifully designed and well-preserved monument in an area filled with modern bars and cafés. Proceed down Veteranen Straße and then Zionskirchstraße until you reach Kastanienallee. Head south on Kastanienallee for 100 meters and then turn left on Fehrbelliner Straße. Continue down Fehrbelliner Straße for 500 meters through the tranquil district down past Teutoburger Platz to Schönhauser Allee.

Turn left on Schönhauser Allee. As you head north, an archway on your left leads up to the Schankhalle Pfefferberg at the former location of one of Berlin's oldest breweries. In the elegant restaurant here, you can see the Schoppe Bräu brew tanks. Passing the Markthalle Pfefferberg, a worthy stop for anyone with an appetite, and HERMAN's Belgian beer bar, take a right at Metzer Straße and carry on until you're greeted by the welcoming arms of Leibhaftig, the home of Wanke Bräu beers.

LEIBHAFTIG

Bringing a contemporary Bavarian touch to the streets of Berlin, Marcus Wanke's elegant streetside restaurant offers a modern twist on traditional cuisine. Along with hearty main dishes, the restaurant specializes in Bavarian tapas, which include handmade dumplings, cold meat plates, patés, and Bergkäse dishes, all packed with flavorful sensations that will leave you craving more. Marcus's personal beer recipes include some traditional Bavarian brewing, focusing on a light complexion and full flavor. Brewed just outside of Berlin and sold exclusively on-site, the craft beers pair perfectly with the home-cooked meals on offer and are changed up to match the seasons. Leibhaftig also offers Schoppe Bräu IPAS for those wanting something more hoppy.

ADDRESS

Leibhaftig
Metzer Straße 30
10405 Berlin
+49 30 54815039
info@leibhaftig.com
www.leibhaftig.com

Photos © Daniel Cole

SOUTH PANKE

BERLIN'S GREEN CORRIDOR THAT CUTS THROUGH THE CITY'S CENTER

MITTE, BERLIN

▷⋯ STARTING POINT	⋯✕ DESTINATION
WEDDING S-BAHN STATION	**THE CASTLE**
🍺 BEER NAME	🀫 DIFFICULTY
BERLINER HOPSCOR PALE ALE	**EASY**
🚃 TRANSPORT	🕐 DURATION
RINGBAHN, U6	**2 H**
⛰ ZONE	↦ LENGTH
A	**5.7 KM**
🔎 HIGHLIGHTS	〰 ELEVATION GAIN
PANKE, INVALIDENPARK, BOROS COLLECTION	ASCENT: 20 M DESCENT: 20 M

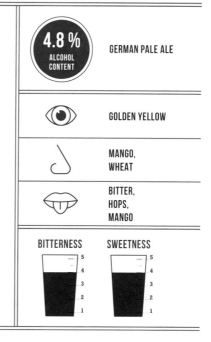

4.8 % ALCOHOL CONTENT	GERMAN PALE ALE
👁	GOLDEN YELLOW
👃	MANGO, WHEAT
👅	BITTER, HOPS, MANGO

BITTERNESS	SWEETNESS
5 4 3 2 1	5 4 3 2 1

BERLINER HOPSCOR PALE ALE. A superb, summery-light craft brew with the right amount of bitterness and a fruity flavor that makes it refreshing without compromising its beer-y essence.

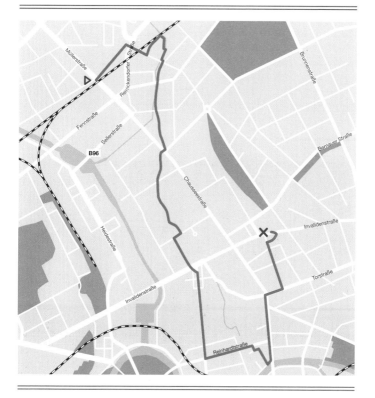

HIKE DESCRIPTION

From Wedding, a hiking trail cuts through the city along the banks of the Panke, extending all the way into the neighboring countryside. Hiking along the Panke and the South Panke is like walking on a secret green avenue right through the middle of the city and all the way to the prominent, bustling neighborhood around Friedrichstraße, where the South Panke joins the Spree.

Leaving the station, head northeast on Lindower Straße through Nettelbeckplatz and cross Reinickendorfer Straße. Then head east on Gerichtstraße. At Gerichtstraße 23, turn into the courtyard, pass the local nightclubs and gyms, and reach the Panke. Turn right and follow the river south into the city center along the footpath on the embankment. The route is marked by blue #5 signs on lampposts.

The #5 route crosses Gerichtstraße and then Schönwalder Straße. After 800 meters, it crosses Schulzendorfer Straße, where the river splits in two. Our path, #5, follows the South Panke to the left just after crossing Schulzendorfer Straße. 300 meters after Schulzendorfer Straße, cross Chausseestraße. The path next weaves through a housing estate and then down through a green corridor filled with wild vegetation.

After 900 meters, turn right on Habersaathstraße and then immediately left on Schwarzer Weg, passing next to Invaliden Park. Leaving the #5, cross Invalidenstraße and head south on Platz vor dem Neuen Tor, following it around to Luisenstraße. Turn right on Luisenstraße. Pass the Charity campus and, after 600 meters, turn left on Reinhardtstraße. Head east for 400 meters, passing the Boros Collection art gallery, which occupies an old war bunker that stands out among the city center shops. Turn right on Am Zirkus and reach the Spree. From here you can see where the South Panke flows into the Spree beneath the promenade.

At the Spree, turn left on Schiffbauerdamm and then left on Friedrich-straße. Head north on Friedrichstraße and then, after 500 meters, take a right onto Torstraße. Turn left on Novalisstraße and then, after 450 meters, right on Invalidenstraße, where you'll come upon the doors of The Castle opening onto the street.

THE CASTLE

Situated just outside the Nordbahnhof, The Castle is like a home away from home. The roomy and welcoming taproom, café, and restaurant emit snug local-pub energy, with leather sofas and a dimly lit interior. In the summer, it's one of the go-to places in Berlin, thanks to a great beer garden that backs out into a luscious green park. It's the owners' third location in the city, and easily their best. The staff are pleasant, and there are up to 20 taps of finely-curated craft beers—including both many local beers featured in this book and The Castle's own Berliner Hopscor. There's also an ample gin selection, and freshly baked pizza is available throughout the day and night.

ADDRESS

The Castle
Invalidenstraße 129
10115 Berlin
+49 30 28047126
www.thecastleberlin.de

Photos © Yvonne Hartmann

EAST BERLIN

EAST SIDE GALLERY

TRAILING THE BERLIN WALL

FRIEDRICHSHAIN,
BERLIN

▷··· STARTING POINT	···✕ DESTINATION
OSTBAHNHOF	**PRIVATBRAUEREI SCHALANDER**
🍺 BEER NAME	🔢 DIFFICULTY
SCHALANDER PILS	**EASY**
🚆 TRANSPORT	🕐 DURATION
S3, S5, S7, S9, RE 1	**30 MIN.**
⛰ ZONE	↦ LENGTH
A	**2.5 KM**
🔍 HIGHLIGHTS	〰 ELEVATION GAIN
BERLIN WALL, OBERBAUMBRÜCKE, WARSCHAUER STRASSE	ASCENT: 10 M DESCENT: 10 M

5.3 % ALCOHOL CONTENT	PILSNER
(eye)	GOLDEN
(nose)	MALTY, HERBY, FLOWERY
(mouth)	MALTY, HERBY

BITTERNESS

5
4
3
2
1

SWEETNESS

5
4
3
2
1

SCHALANDER PILS. A golden pilsner with a malty, slightly bitter kick and a mild hoppy aftertaste.

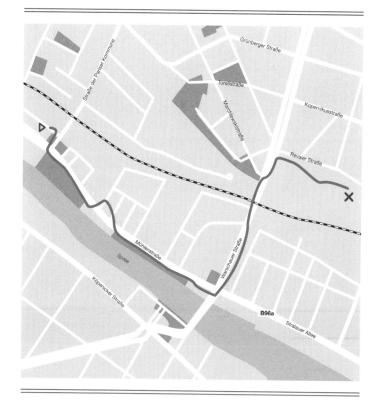

HIKE DESCRIPTION

No visit to the German capital is complete without seeing at least some of the Berlin Wall. The East Side Gallery in Friedrichshain is the longest remaining strip of the Wall left in Berlin. Today, it serves as a testament to the past as well as functioning as an open-air art gallery. At just over a kilometer in length, the gallery presents messages of peace, depictions of iconic cultural moments, and memorabilia, providing a colorful view into the city's past.

As you head out of the main entrance of the Ostbahnhof station, turn first left and then immediately right onto Straße der Pariser Kommune. Crossing Mühlenstraße, you'll arrive at the East Side Gallery, which you'll follow in an easterly direction along the river. Walking along the Wall at a leisurely pace, take time to view all the modern murals created by the global array of artists who originally worked on the gallery back in the 1990s.

You can also walk on the other side of the Wall, where a park runs along the river. In summer, this side is often filled with people looking out across the water, drinking beer, or playing with their dogs.

At the end of the gallery, you'll come to the Oberbaumbrücke on your right. Instead of crossing this bridge, however, head in the opposite direction and up Warschauer Straße. After passing the East Side Mall, you'll walk across the Warschauerbrücke, which provides epic views toward the city center as trains whiz by below.

After a few hundred meters, you'll reach a traffic light. Cross over Warschauer Straße and head north for 20 meters until you reach a bratwurst restaurant. To the side of this take-away joint are a set of metallic stairs that drop down into the subcultural domain known as RAW-Gelände, a

post-modern melee of underground clubs, restaurants, and galleries. Follow the cobbled streets and old industrial rail line eastward, past the skating hall, climbing center, and antiques warehouse, to the very end of the strip, where the lights of Schalander will invite you in.

PRIVATBRAUEREI SCHALANDER

In traditional breweries, "Schalander" is the name given to the part of the brewery where workers chill out and relax. This is exactly the vibe and demeanor of this intimate microbrewery. Privatbrauerei Schalander's outstanding feature is a huge garden that looks out across the old industrial community estate. The bar sells three fresh beers all year round—a Pilsner, a Dunkel, and a Weizen—along with a variety of seasonal offerings. The team have been brewing in Berlin for several years, but after their main restaurant closed, they settled in this postindustrial location, which has a feel of being traditional and urban at the same time. There are bar snacks available, including Flammkuchen and pretzels, and with the amount of food options available elsewhere in the area, finding something to eat will never be a problem.

ADDRESS

Privatbrauerei Schalander
Revaler Straße 99, Haus 9
10245 Berlin
+49 30 94512299
info@schalander-berlin.de
www.schalander-berlin.de

Photos © Daniel Cole

KARL-MARX-ALLEE

A SOVIET SIGHTSEEING VOYAGE

FRIEDRICHSHAIN, BERLIN

▷··· STARTING POINT	···✕ DESTINATION
SCHILLINGSTRASSE U-BAHN STATION	**HOPS & BARLEY**
🍺 BEER NAME	DIFFICULTY
FRIEDRICHSHAINER PILSNER	**EASY**
🚊 TRANSPORT	⏲ DURATION
U5	**45 MIN.**
⛰ ZONE	⊢ LENGTH
A	**3.5 KM**
🔍 HIGHLIGHTS	〰 ELEVATION GAIN
KINO INTERNATIONAL, STRAUSBERGER PLATZ, FRANKFURTER TOR, BOXHAGENER PLATZ	ASCENT: 0 M DESCENT: 0 M

 PILSNER

 HAZY GOLDEN,
WHITE HEAD

 CITRUS,
HOPS

 MALTS,
CITRUS

BITTERNESS   SWEETNESS

 FRIEDRICHSHAINER PILSNER. A bright yet slightly malty clean pils
with a mild fruit aftertaste.

HIKE DESCRIPTION

A boulevard of forgotten dreams, the wide and majestic Karl-Marx-Allee, with its grandiose Soviet architecture, is evocative of a time long past. Built as a shining example of Soviet pride, the once-luxurious apartment blocks that line the former city entrance—previously known as Stalinallee—are today best known from their appearances in film and TV shows, including *Good Bye Lenin!*, *The Lives of Others*, and *The Queen's Gambit*. The ever-changing architecture along this iconic piece of history reveals a city in constant flux, with GDR-era restaurants and modern workspaces co-existing side by side.

Since the fall of the Berlin Wall, Friedrichshain has become one of the best districts in the city for craft beer breweries and taprooms. Within just a 2-kilometer radius, you'll find some of the city's best beers and establishments, some of which, like Straßenbrau and Schalander, have their own pages in this book.

Leaving the station, head east on Karl-Marx-Allee, taking note of Kino International to your left and Café Moskau in front of you.

Crossing Strausberger Platz—shadowed by towering apartment buildings—carry on along Karl-Marx-Allee for 2.5 kilometers until you reach the Frankfurter Tor. Along the way, you'll pass several historic landmarks, including Café Sibylle, the Karl-Marx-Allee rose garden, and the former Kosmos cinema.

When you reach the remarkable domed towers of Frankfurter Tor, cross Warschauer Straße and then, turning right, follow it south past the neighborhood BrewDog branch. Turn left on Boxhagener Straße and follow it for 500 meters, passing the Protokoll Berlin taproom, till you reach

Gabriel-Max-Straße. Turn right on Gabriel-Max-Straße and proceed for 350 meters, passing Boxhagener Park. Turn left on Wühlischstraße. Soon you'll be greeted by the streetside signs of Hops & Barley.

HOPS & BARLEY

Located in an old butcher's shop, this little brewery, with its rich and vibrant beers, has developed a reputation as one of Berlin's best. As a bar, it's Berlin through-and-through, with pub snacks on offer, football games in the evening, a smoking room in the back, and an abundance of local staff eager to top your glass up at any time. It's a home away from home for many locals, who have sworn by its hospitality for over a decade—this writer included!

In addition to its regular tap beers—Pilsner, Dunkel, and Weizen—the Hops and Barley team offer an excellent cider, fizzing with natural character. Their specials are also awash with quality, among them a must-try Bernstein.

ADDRESS

Hops & Barley
Wühlischstraße 22–23
10245 Berlin
+49 30 29367534
www.hopsandbarley.eu

Photos © Daniel Cole

GÖRLITZER PARK

ALONG THE TRACKS TO BERLIN'S HIPPEST INDOOR FOOD MARKET

KREUZBERG, BERLIN

▷··· STARTING POINT	···✕ DESTINATION
TREPTOWER PARK S-BAHN STATION	**HEIDENPETERS**
🍺 BEER NAME	🔠 DIFFICULTY
PALE ALE	**EASY**
🚋 TRANSPORT	🕐 DURATION
RINGBAHN, S8, S9, S41, S42, S85	**45 MIN.**
⛰ ZONE	↦ LENGTH
A	**3.3 KM**
🔍 HIGHLIGHTS	〰 ELEVATION GAIN
GÖRLITZER PARK	ASCENT: 10 M DESCENT: 10 M

5.6 % ALCOHOL CONTENT	PALE ALE
👁	YELLOW, ORANGE
👃	CITRUS, SPICY, FLOWERS
👄	FRUITY, HOPS, CARAMEL

BITTERNESS

5
4
3
2
1

SWEETNESS

5
4
3
2
1

 PALE ALE. Fruity and exotic, this crisp and hoppy pale ale has an abundant flavor profile and triggers an explosion of taste on the tongue.

HIKE DESCRIPTION

Take a walk through history along the former railway tracks that once connected Berlin to Vienna. Today, this repurposed land is home to Görlitzer Park, a vast green space filled with sports pitches where locals can enjoy some well-earned downtime. Remnants of the park's past are visible throughout, with the station's remaining platform now home to a café and bar. Some of the line's old steel tracks have been twisted into an arching commemorative monument.

From the station, turn to the left and head southwest on Elsenstraße for 750 meters until you reach the steel bridge where the railway once ran. Follow the set of stairs up to the bridge, cross Elsenstraße, and follow the footpath along the former tracks for 800 meters, all the way to Görlitzer Brücke, which crosses Landwehr Canal. When the Berlin Wall was erected, it divided the two sides of the canal, eventually leading to the demise of the railway line that once ran across the water.

As you cross Görlitzer Brücke and enter Görlitzer Park, there's a mound on your left where a railway-turntable once stood. Moving on further and merging into the perpetual traffic of pedestrians, you'll reach a deep cavity in the park where a tunnel once ran beneath the two sides of the former railway. In the summer, this basin is often full of musicians, frisbee enthusiasts, and young people drinking in the sunshine.

Continuing past the remnants of the station platform on your right, cross Skalitzer Straße, pass the Emmaus-Kirche, and walk across Lausitzer Platz to Eisenbahnstraße to your right. Follow Eisenbahnstraße for 100 meters and reach the entrance of Markthalle Neun on the left-hand side. This community-run center is filled with local providers of fruit, vegetables, and other foods with a tilt toward sustainable

production and organic growing. Walk through this buzzing hive of snack-tivity, past the pulled-pork barbeque restaurant, pasta emporium, and organic vegetable market, and arrive at the Heidenpeters beer stand, tucked away on the side next to a seating area and sporting a gleaming handmade sign and wooden decor.

HEIDENPETERS

The brewery and bar established by Johannes Heidenpeter is in a 100-year-old traditional market hall that is now regularly filled with local fresh-food markets and street-food vendors. Although small, this little beer corner is just the tip of Heidenpeters' brewing world, connecting the business's headquarters in the basement below to a city-wide distribution network. Heidenpeters sets itself apart with its colorful logos and fantastic array of beers, which includes the ever-popular Thirsty Lady (blond ale), Pilz (Pilsner), and many more. The brewery regularly surprises the locals with its mixed selection of seasonal drinks; a multitude of bocks and pale ales find their way to the taproom over the course of the year.

ADDRESS

Heidenpeters Brauerei
Eisenbahnstraße 41–42
10997 Berlin
+49 176 2229188
mail@heidenpeters.de
www.heidenpeters.de

Photos © Yvonne Hartmann

TREPTOWER PARK

DINOSAURS, SOVIETS & EINSTEIN: ALL IN ONE PARK

ALT-TREPTOW, BERLIN

▷⋯ STARTING POINT	⋯✗ DESTINATION
TREPTOWER PARK S-BAHN STATION	**BERLINER BERG BRAUEREI**
🍺 BEER NAME	🎲 DIFFICULTY
BERLINER WEISSE	**MODERATE**
🚆 TRANSPORT	🕐 DURATION
S8, S9, S41, S42, S47, S85	**1.5 H**
⛰ ZONE	↦ LENGTH
A	**7.5 KM**
🔍 HIGHLIGHTS	〰 ELEVATION GAIN
SPREEPARK, ARCHENHOLD OBSERVATORY, SOVIET MEMORIAL	ASCENT: 10 M DESCENT: 10 M

BERLINER WEISSE

HAZY,
GOLDEN

FLOWERY,
FRESH FRUIT,
HERBAL

SOUR,
CITRUS,
SWEET

BITTERNESS	SWEETNESS

 BERLINER WEISSE. A traditional sweet and flowery Berliner Weiße with an abundance of colorful flavors that will leave you gasping for more.

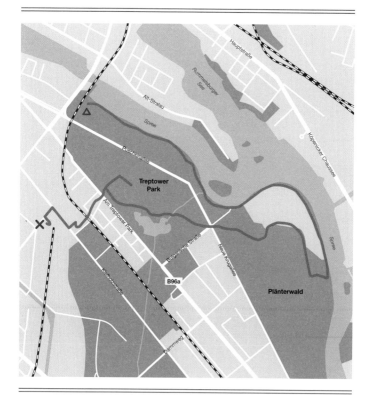

HIKE DESCRIPTION

Adjoining the River Spree, Treptower Park and the neighboring Plänterwald feature an abundance of cultural oddities, historical monuments, beer gardens, outdoor cinemas, water-sports facilities, and much else to take your mind away from everyday life. During the summer months, the park is abuzz with locals playing sports, sitting by the water, and kayaking in rental boats. At the same time, the park and nearby woodlands hide several important artifacts from the country's history, including a colossal Soviet memorial, Germany's oldest observatory—once frequented by Albert Einstein—and a deserted theme park with an ominous past.

Leaving the station via the riverside exit, follow the signposts that lead straight ahead to the harborside, a stretch of land full of international food stalls, bars, and charter boat wharfs. Follow the waterside in an easterly direction for a kilometer, making your way through the park that looks across to the Stralauer peninsula on the other side of the water.

As the path bends along the river, it eventually passes Zenner, a wonderfully preserved 200-year-old restaurant, beer garden, and event space that offers stunning views across the water. There you'll see the Insel der Jugend (Island of Youth), a quiet spot where city residents can often be seen relaxing and enjoying the serenity, and where you can rent kayaks and watch outdoor movies during the summer months.

Following the river further, under the Abteibrücke and past the moored boat-restaurants, the path leads to Plänterwald, a woodland area beside the river. As you walk along the waterside, a fenced-off abandoned theme park starts to appear on your right. Spreepark was once a bustling attraction with a Ferris wheel and dinosaur statues, and its tragic demise has left the area in disrepair for decades. Nowadays, you can still make out old carnival rides and water features among the ruins.

From the Insel der Jugend, a 1.8-kilometer walk along the river's edge features views straight into the heart of the city. Follow the riverside path around the park until you reach the renovated Eierhäuschen, which was a restaurant in the 19th century. Just beyond this, turn right on the forest path that heads back into the woodlands, which, after 200 meters, leads to a concrete footpath. Follow this footpath to the right as it gradually turns into a road, Wasserweg, that circles around to the back of Spreepark, where you'll pass the visitor's entrance. After a kilometer, you'll arrive at a three-way junction, where the entrance to the old amusement park used to stand. From here, follow the path to the left into the woods down the old entrance road. After 200 meters, take a right into the woods and continue for 500 meters until the woodland path emerges at the junction of Alt-Treptower and Bulgarische Straße.

Cross directly over Bulgarische Straße and, on the left side of the junction, follow the footpath into the opening in the woods. As you follow the footpath, you'll pass Archenhold-Sternwarte on your right. This is Germany's oldest and largest observatory telescope and a place where Albert Einstein used to give lectures. The last part of the path leads to a junction at the back of the fenced-off Soviet memorial. Follow the path that leads to the left as it hugs the Karpfenteich pond, a beautiful and isolated body of water surrounded by idyllic picnic spots.

As you reach the end of the pond, follow the path to the left of the Kita (Kindergarten) as it wends its way back through the park. After 300 meters, you'll arrive at a gate, passing through which you'll reach the arched entrance to the Soviet Memorial, where a cobbled road will take you into the historic area. Built at the end of the Second World War, the expansive memorial is adorned with statues and graves that commemorate the 80,000 Red Army soldiers who lost their lives retaking Berlin. The immense space is filled with Soviet sarcophagi and granite flags and looks out over the gardens below. Overlooking the cemetery is a colossal 12-meter-tall bronze statue of a Russian soldier clutching a German child and sword while crushing a swastika under his feet.

Turn back, exit the memorial, and head toward the memorial entrance at Am Treptower Park. To the left is a crossing that will take you straight onto Puderstraße. Follow Puderstraße for 300 meters and then, after you pass beneath the railway bridge, turn right onto Kiefholzstraße. Follow Kiefholzstraße for another 300 meters, crossing over the yet-to-be-finished highway, and reach Treptower Straße on your left. Turn onto Treptower Straße; after 20 meters, you'll reach the brewery and beer garden on the left.

BERLINER BERG BRAUEREI

Since bursting onto the scene in 2016, Berliner Berg beer has found its way into many of the city's best bars. Producing a mix of IPAs, Pilsners, and Lagers, Berliner Berg is best known for its amazing Berliner Weiße, an incredible modern take on the classic drink that somehow manages to combine many flavors into a single beverage. The beer garden and brewery are adorned in traditional fresh green colors, and dense foliage offers a refreshing reprieve to the surrounding industrial area. Food trucks often offer meals on the weekend, but the owners encourage you to bring your own snacks to enjoy with your brew. You can book brewery tours online, and in the evenings there are sometimes outdoor film screenings.

ADDRESS

Berliner Berg Brauerei
Treptower Straße 39
12059 Berlin
+49 30 64435906
info@berlinerberg.de
www.berlinerberg.com

Photos © Yvonne Hartmann

VOLKSPARK FRIEDRICHSHAIN

FROM PRENZLAUER BERG TO THE BUNKERBERG

FRIEDRICHSHAIN, BERLIN

▷⋯ STARTING POINT	⋯✕ DESTINATION
SENEFELDERPLATZ U-BAHN STATION	**BRAUEREI FLESSA**
🍺 BEER NAME	🎴 DIFFICULTY
MANDARINA	**MODERATE**
🚊 TRANSPORT	🕐 DURATION
U2	**1.5 H**
⛰ ZONE	↦ LENGTH
A	**7 KM**
🔎 HIGHLIGHTS	〰 ELEVATION GAIN
PRENZLAUER BERG WATER TOWER, MÄRCHENBRUNNEN, GREAT BUNKERBERG FRIEDRICHSHAIN, VELODROME	ASCENT: 40 M DESCENT: 40 M

5.0 % ALCOHOL CONTENT	RED LAGER
👁	CLOUDY COPPER-BROWN
👃	ORANGE FRUIT, WHEAT
👄	BITTER, MALT, FRUIT

BITTERNESS
SWEETNESS

MANDARINA. A bitter and dry red lager with subtly sweet notes of mandarin and a mild caramel aftertaste.

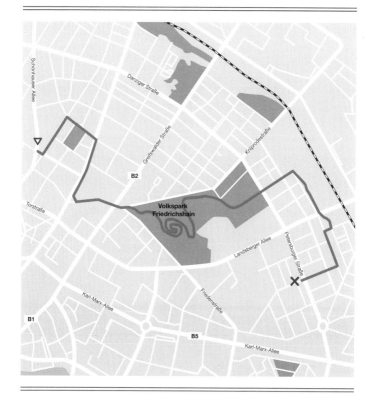

HIKE DESCRIPTION

Volkspark Friedrichshain has almost everything you could want from an open public space. There's an open-air cinema, a running track, baroque fountains, an abundance of table-tennis sets, and a beautiful lakeside restaurant. There are also artworks, historical statues, and remnants of a demolished Second World War bunker. The park's energy can be felt day and night, with locals hanging out, going on strolls, and gathering around barbecues.

Leaving the station, head north on Kollwitzstraße for 600 meters into the flamboyant district of Prenzlauer Berg; then head east on Knaackstraße, passing the Prenzlauer Berg Water Tower.

After 350 meters, head south on Prenzlauer Allee and then take a left on Prenzlauer Berg, cross Greifswalder Straße, and head directly into Volkspark Friedrichshain. Just inside the park is the Märchenbrunnen, a neo-baroque fountain with fairy-tale statues.

Passing the fountains, take the second right (heading southeast) and arrive at the Großer Bunkerberg, the site of a flak tower constructed during the Second World War. Unlike the tower in Volkspark Humboldthain, this one has been demolished and is now merely a mound of rubble you can ascend to gain a view across the neighborhood.

After climbing the Großer Bunkerberg, head downward in a clockwise direction, pass the statue of Frederick II, and take the second path to the left past the lake and the old GDR restaurant Schoenbrunn. Head clockwise around the restaurant, taking the second right turn. After 200 meters, take the path to the right over the hill and past the war memorial. Go down the stairs from the memorial, turn right, proceed for 150 meters, and then turn left and head into the park's eastern quarter.

Carry on past the climbing wall and the volleyball fields for 300 meters and over to Danziger Straße. Cross Danziger Straße and continue eastward on Paul-Heyse-Straße to the Velodrom, a mighty, modern, circular events hall. Climb the stairs to the top of the Velodrom and head south through the park situated on top of the events space. After 400 meters, return to street level, cross Landsberger Allee, and continue along Hausburgstraße. Turn right on Straßmannstraße and follow it to Petersburger Straße, where you'll see the sign for Brauerei Flessa on your right.

BRAUEREI FLESSA

This secluded neighborhood brewery is tucked away inside the courtyard of an apartment building. Lucky neighbors, right? Outside, next to the names of the residents, there's a bell that grants access to this hidden local gem. Although there's no taproom, visitors are welcome to swing by at any time and pick up some fresh chilled beers straight from Christoph Flessa's very local brewery. Flessa also offers brewing classes, which have picked up some extremely positive reviews. Flessa beers can be found in a multitude of local bars and restaurants, with a Pilsner, IPA, Weizen, Mandarina, and Extra Ale available throughout the year.

ADDRESS

Brauerei Flessa
Petersburger Straße 39
10249 Berlin
+49 30 23409269
www.brauerei flessa.de

Photos © Yvonne Hartmann

WATER CITY STROLL

FROM THE INDUSTRIAL HEARTLAND OF BREWING
TO THE FUTURE OF BEER

TREPTOW,
BERLIN

▷··· STARTING POINT	···✕ DESTINATION
TREPTOWER PARK S-BAHN STATION	**STRASSENBRÄU TAPROOM**
🍺 BEER NAME	DIFFICULTY
STRALAUER PILS	**EASY**
🚃 TRANSPORT	🕐 DURATION
S9, S9, S41, S42, S49, S85	**1 H 15 MIN.**
🏔 ZONE	↦ LENGTH
A	**6.3 KM**
🔍 HIGHLIGHTS	〜 ELEVATION GAIN
DORFKIRCHE STRALAU, STRALAU SPREETUNNEL, RUMMELSBURGER BUCHT	ASCENT: 10 M DESCENT: 10 M

5.0 % ALCOHOL CONTENT	PILSNER
	LIGHT GOLD
	LIGHT HERBS AND MALT
	HERBY, BITTER, FLOWERY

BITTERNESS
5
4
3
2
1

SWEETNESS
5
4
3
2
1

STRALAUER PILS. This light and refreshing ale-like pilsner features herbal notes and has a whole lot of character.

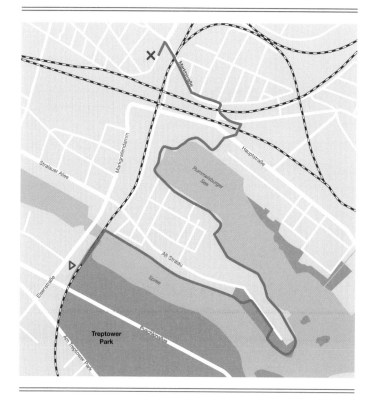

HIKE DESCRIPTION

The Stralau peninsula is an island of calm in the otherwise chaotic area that connects Friedrichshain to Neukölln. Indeed, Stralau was a small fishing village before eventually integrating into the Berlin fold. Walking around the calm and secluded Stralau peninsula provides a sense of serenity and incredible views down the Spree.

During the 1800s, the Stralau peninsula became a hub for the industrial revolution, and several factory facades still survive—including that of an old bottling factory that served one of the city's largest breweries. Leave the station through the park entrance and then turn left and head north across the Spree on Parkwegbrücke.

Take the stairs down to the water on your right after you cross the bridge and follow the waterside Spreeufer path as it heads counterclockwise around the peninsula, looking out to Treptower Park on the other side of the water.

After a kilometer, the path snakes around the Dorfkirche (village church), the relic of a building dating back to 1464 (the oldest in Friedrichshain/Kreuzberg). Follow the path for another 200 meters, where the ground starts to dip to the left. This is what is left of an old tram tunnel that once ran beneath the river, connecting the area to the park on the other side.

Rounding the peninsula and heading back on the other side along Uferweg, the path takes you past numerous quaint boathouses and the floating Kap Frida café, a perfect spot for a break. After a few hundred meters, the path passes an old, red-brick former palm-oil factory. Round the bay for another kilometer as the footpath turns into Paul-und-Paula-Ufer. Turn left onto Hauptstraße, pass the table-tennis

courts, and reach the main road, also called Hauptstraße. Cross Hauptstraße and take the pathway directly in front of you, heading through the Rummelsburg S-Bahn Station onto Nöldnerstraße.

Turn left on Nöldnerstraße and right on Karlshorster Straße, which bends to the left and becomes Marktstraße. Take Marktstraße (which turns into Boxhagenerstraße) for 500 meters straight through Victoriastadt until you arrive at the junction with Neue Bahnhofstraße, with Victoria Stadler—a bright and charming little neighborhood brewery—on the corner. Head south (left) on Neue Bahnhofstraße until you come to the Straßenbräu Taproom to the right.

STRASSENBRÄU TAPROOM

This modern and elegantly styled craft-beer bar is chic and homely, with ample seating to make you feel at ease while working your way through its extensive menu. It specializes in flavorful IPAs, Weizens, and Pilsners (the long-running Sonnenallee is another highly praised choice!), all made with love. Straßenbräu's knack for perfecting savory beers has won it an army of local fans. There's no food menu, but the team is happy for you to bring in anything you can find in the neighboring restaurants, and you can enjoy it all sitting inside or out.

ADDRESS

Straßenbräu Taproom
Neue Bahnhofstraße 30
10245 Berlin
+49 33 17043211
www.strassenbraeu.de

Photos © Daniel Cole

MÜGGELSEE

LAKES, BEACHES & FORESTS

FRIEDRICHSHAGEN, BERLIN

▷⋯ STARTING POINT	⋯✕ DESTINATION
FRIEDRICHSHAGEN S-BAHN STATION	**BRAU- UND GENUSSWERKSTATT BERLIN-FRIEDRICHSHAGEN**
🍺 BEER NAME	🀱 DIFFICULTY
DOLLE MOLLE KUPFERSAMT	**HARD**
🚃 TRANSPORT	🕐 DURATION
S3	**4 H**
⛰ ZONE	↦ LENGTH
B	**18.3 KM**
🔎 HIGHLIGHTS	〰 ELEVATION GAIN
SPREETUNELL, RAHNSDORF, STRANDBAND MÜGGELSEE, WASSERWERKSMUSEUM	ASCENT: 100 M DESCENT: 100 M

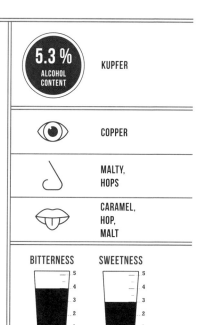

5.3 % ALCOHOL CONTENT	KUPFER
👁	COPPER
👃	MALTY, HOPS
👄	CARAMEL, HOP, MALT

BITTERNESS   **SWEETNESS**

DOLLE MOLLE KUPFERSAMT. A tasty and aromatic caramel-flavored beer with a subtle bitterness and a well-rounded hoppy character.

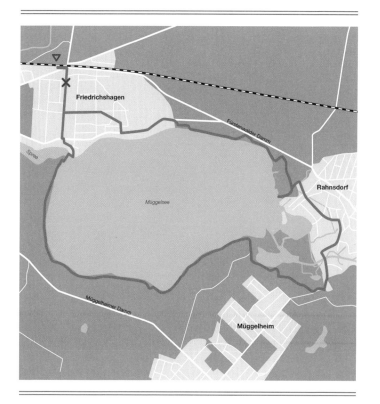

HIKE DESCRIPTION

The 4-kilometer-long Müggelsee in Berlin's eastern districts is surrounded by lush woodlands and features several secluded sandy beaches and waterside restaurants. It's easily one of Berlin's most beautiful bodies of water. With an abundance of forest trails, bike routes, and boat rental spots, there's plenty to do if just plain swimming doesn't sound entertaining enough for you. But remember: if you're coming during the summer months, swimwear and beach gear is a must!

Leaving the station, head south on Bölschestraße for just over a kilometer. Turn left on Müggelseedamm and then right on Scharnweberstraße, following the signs to the Spreetunnel. Head through the impressive underwater tunnel and follow the water's edge in a counterclockwise direction for 6 kilometers. Just before you reach the end of the lakeside path at Müggelhort, turn right and head away from the lake on Straße zum Müggelhort. After 150 meters, turn left on the footpath, signposted toward Erkner, which leads to the Kleiner Müggelsee. After a few hundred meters, you'll see a giant sandy beach on your left that looks across to opulent houses on the other side of the lake.

Carry on along the forest path eastward for 800 meters, turn left on Zu den Müggelheimer Wiesen, and then left again on Zur Fähre. At the end of the road, you'll be greeted by a man in a rowboat who will ferry you across to the other side of the Müggelspree for the price of a short-journey ticket. This tiny waterway service has been in operation for over 100 years, but only runs between May and October on weekends and public holidays.

You'll now find yourself just outside the quaint 14th-century fishing village of Hahnsdorf, which introduces itself with a traditional smoked-fish restaurant. Carry on into the village and swing round the church and through the charming streets. At the end of Dorfstraße, turn left on Lachsfang and then left again on Aalsteig, which then becomes Wiesenstraße. After 750 meters, turn right on Seestraße and then immediately left on Brückenstraße. Follow Brückenstraße for 200 meters and then

take a left on a woodland path after crossing the Fredersdorfer Mühlen-fließ. After 150 meters, the path veers off to the right. Just before it hits Fürstenwalder Damm, a side path heads off to the left, with signposts pointing toward Fisch-Borke, a lakeside beer garden. From the beer garden, follow the lakeside path counterclockwise once more onto the Strandbad Müggelsee, following the sandy beach all the way around to the FKK (nudist) enclosure.

Follow the path to the north of the FKK beach, carrying on counter-clockwise along the lakeshore and passing through the beautiful and remote Nordstrand beach. The path eventually ends at Müggelseedam. Follow Müggelseedamm in a westerly direction for a kilometer, passing the Waterworks Museum on your left. Take a right on Kalkseestraße and then a left on Rahnsdorfer Straße. Follow Rahnsdorfer Straße for a kilometer and reach Bölschestraße again. Turn right on Bölschestraße and follow it northward for 400 meters, at which point the Rathaus and Ratskeller will be on your left.

BRAU- & GENUSSWERKSTATT BERLIN-FRIEDRICHSHAGEN

Once a holiday village and now a sprightly and chic Berlin suburb, Friedrichshagen used to be the home of the giant Bürger-Bräu brewery, whose empty premises still stand beside the waters of the Müggelsee. Stepping in to fill the gap left by Bürger-Bräu's demise, a group of locals set themselves up in the old town hall, brewing Friedrichshagen Dolle Molle beer and serving it in the antiquated setting. Recently restored to its former glory, with rediscovered classical murals on the walls, the Ratskeller has a great deal of old-timey, classical Brauhaus charm. With two beers regularly on offer, a Pilsner and a Kupfer, as well as homemade schnapps and real pub food, there is everything you could ever need here.

ADDRESS

Brau- & Genusswerkstatt Berlin-Friedrichshagen AG
Bölschestraße 87–88
12587 Berlin
+49 30 64091227
post@brauerei-friedrichshagen.de
www.brauerei-friedrichshagen.de

Photos © Yvonne Hartmann

RIXDORF

A HIDDEN BOHEMIAN VILLAGE IN THE HEART OF THE METROPOLIS

NEUKÖLLN, BERLIN

▷⋯ STARTING POINT	⋯✗ DESTINATION
HERMANNPLATZ U-BAHN STATION	**ROTBART**
🍺 BEER NAME	🔐 DIFFICULTY
ROTBART ROTBIER	**EASY**
🚃 TRANSPORT	🕐 DURATION
U7, U8	**1 H 15 MIN.**
🗻 ZONE	↦ LENGTH
A	**5 KM**
🔍 HIGHLIGHTS	〰 ELEVATION GAIN
RATHAUS NEUKÖLLN, BERLINER KINDLER BRAUEREI, KÖRNERPARK	ASCENT: 20 M DESCENT: 20 M

ROTBIER

DARK,
RED BROWN

MALTY,
CHOCOLATE,
FOREST FRUITS

CARAMEL,
OAK,
ROASTED MALT

BITTERNESS

SWEETNESS

 ROTBART ROTBIER. Tart and almost chocolatey in taste, this malty and well-balanced brew has a wood-chip aftertaste reminiscent of an oaky whiskey.

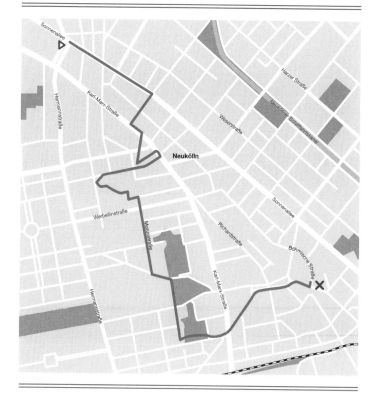

HIKE DESCRIPTION

The former Bohemian village of Rixdorf is hidden between two hectic roads, Sonnenallee and Karl-Marx-Straße. As you enter the leafy neighborhood, you'll come upon cobbled roads, historical buildings, and huge open courtyards; around Richardplatz, the village square, you'll see ancient churches, forges, and coach houses. It's like taking a step back in time. The old village is filled with neighborhood bars, boutiques, and a serenity that its inhabitants clearly relish.

Start at the Hermannplatz exit and head east on Sonnenallee amid the hustle and bustle of everyday Neukölln life. This is easily one of the busiest districts in town, and the locals bounce from vegetable shops to cafés, boutique retailers to butchers. Neukölln is home to a large community of people of Turkish descent, and the area is filled with Middle Eastern eateries, bazaar-like shops, and cafés.

After 750 meters, turn right at Weichselstraße, pass jaja (one of Berlin's best organic wine restaurants), and arrive in front of the Neukölln-Arcaden, from the top of which you'll be rewarded with great views of the city. Turn left on Karl-Marx-Straße and follow it until you reach the Rathaus Neukölln.

At the Rathaus Neukölln, turn right on Boddinstraße and then, after 500 meters, turn left on Mainzer Straße. Turn almost immediately left on Am Sudhaus to arrive at the old Kindl brewery, now an arts center. Look inside to view the huge copper tanks; then grab a Rollberg beer, which is brewed just next door. Head south for 20 meters and turn left on Werbellinstraße and then right on Morusstraße.

Head south on Morusstraße for 500 meters and proceed through the cemetery and directly onward into Körnerpark, a palatial baroque garden fitted with lush green spaces, ornamental fountains, and well-kept flower beds.

Leave Körnerpark on the south side on Schierker Straße, head east and cross Karl-Marx-Straße, and then proceed down Kirchhofstraße to Richard-platz. Soak up the 18th-century village vibes: visit the huge courtyards where horses were once kept, the old forgery that is still open today, and the Bethlehem Church, which dates to the 15th century.

Go down Schudomastraße to Böhmischer Platz, a square filled with bohemian young people playing music and table tennis. Here you'll also find the Rotbart bar, the life and soul of this humble little village.

ROTBART

This bustling cozy corner bar is typical of the type of neighborhood establishments you find in Berlin. Second-hand furniture, rustic home-made decor, plaster-free walls, and candlelight provide the ambiance and energy of a chic and well-loved local hangout, reminiscent of 1990s Berlin. The bar is well stocked and serves everything from cock-tails to wines, and the bar owners initially turned to the local brewing team at Bier Fabrik for beer. Bier Fabrik was later taken over by Brewer's Tribute, one of Berlin's best independent craft beer companies. For Rotbart (that's "red beard" in English), they created something that matched not just the name of the bar, but its vibe as well—hence the beer's special notes of oak and well-balanced flavor. The beer is a real one-of-a-kind, just like the bar it is brewed for.

ADDRESS

Rotbart
Böhmische Straße 43
12055 Berlin
+49 30 49080740
www.rotbart-rixdorf.de

Photos © Yvonne Hartmann

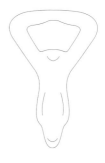

HERZBERGE

AN ADVENTURE THROUGH EAST BERLIN

LICHTENBERG, BERLIN

▷⋯ STARTING POINT	⋯✕ DESTINATION
FRIEDRICHSFELDE-OST S-BAHN STATION	**PROTOKOLL**
🍺 BEER NAME	🁢 DIFFICULTY
RESEARCH CHEMICALS	**MODERATE**
🚆 TRANSPORT	🕐 DURATION
S5, S7, S75	**3.5 H**
⛰ ZONE	↦ LENGTH
B	**12 KM**
🔍 HIGHLIGHTS	〰 ELEVATION GAIN
LANDSCHAFTSPARK HERZBERGE, DONG XUAN CENTER, LICHTENBERG PARK, SAMARITERKIRCHE	ASCENT: 40 M DESCENT: 90 M

8.0 % ALCOHOL CONTENT	DNEIPA
(eye icon)	DARK ORANGE
(nose icon)	CITRUS, HOPPY
(mouth icon)	ORANGE, CITRUS, HOPS

BITTERNESS	SWEETNESS
5 4 3 2 1	5 4 3 2 1

 RESEARCH CHEMICALS. A wonderfully crafted hazy IPA that excites with its fruity aroma and provides a tasting experience full of exotic zings and twangs.

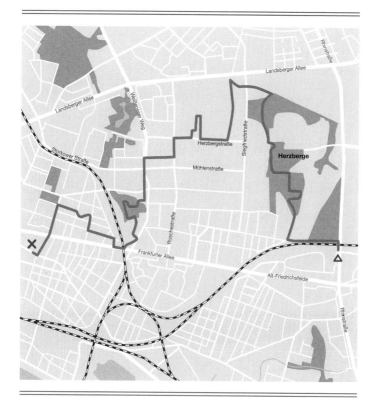

HIKE DESCRIPTION

In the heart of the eastern district of Lichtenberg, amidst the industrial warehouses and high-rise buildings, is a landscape of green fields and farm animals. The Landschaftspark Herzberge is an urban-agriculture area where Pomeranian sheep trim the untamed grass and an organic agri-business has set up shop growing seasonal vegetables. Established along a former railway line, the Herzberge park is part of a wider effort to regenerate the former industrial area, bringing more nature and color into the eastern part of Berlin.

Leaving the station, head north on Rhinstraße. After a few hundred meters, take the steps down to the left and follow the path between the private gardens and the rail tracks.

200 meters along the path, take a right after the Memorial of the Socialists and follow the old railway bed northward alongside the cemetery. The wooded path eventually reaches the Stadtgarten's allotted grounds and paths, weaving through vegetable patches and open fields.

Walk through the urban agricultural grounds for one kilometer in a northerly direction between the fields and the woodlands until you reach the hospital (Evangelisches Krankenhaus Königin Elisabeth Herzberge). Then head west on Herzbergstraße and almost immediately turn north onto the old railway footpath, skirting the protected livestock field to the right. At the end of the footpath, head west across Siegfriedstraße, pass through the private allotments, and then go south, turning left on Am Wasserwerk back to Herzbergstraße.

Heading west, Herzbergstraße passes the Dong Xuan Center, a series of warehouses specializing in Asian goods. Continue to the west before turning left on Möllendorffstraße. After one kilometer on Möllendorffstraße, take a right into Volkspark Lichtenberg with its paths, ponds, and concourses. Exit the park next to the Parkaue Theater on the south side of the park.

Head south on Parkaue and then turn left on Deutschmeisterstraße and right on Möllendorffstraße. Turn right on Frankfurter Allee and after 800 meters, turn right on Voigtstraße. Follow Voigtstraße for about 300 meters and then turn left on Bänschstraße. After 200 meters, Bänschstraße passes around the Samariterkirche, a center of the 1980s East German peace movement.

After 300 meters, take a left on Proskauer Straße. After 400 meters, Proskauer Straße turns into Niederbarnimstraße. Continue on Niederbarnimstraße for another 300 meters and then take a right on Boxhagener Straße. You'll soon see Protokoll on the right side of the street.

PROTOKOLL

A real paradise for beer nerds, the immaculately designed taproom at Protokoll excels in showcasing exemplary brews from Germany and around the world. From the 24 taps or the abundant bottle fridge, you can feast on a selection of IPAs, Weizen, Gueuze beers, and much more. The rotating taps feature an ever-evolving selection of manifestations from Protokoll's new brewery, a kaleidoscopic meeting of mixed-variety craft IPAs. A regular haunt for beer lovers and locals, the bar itself is always packed, and although there's no food menu, in Friedrichshain you're never far away from something great to eat.

ADDRESS

Protokoll
Boxhagener Straße 110
10245 Berlin
+49 33 17043211
hello@protokollberlin.de
www.protokollberlin.de

Photos © Daniel Cole

WUHLE VALLEY TRAIL

WHERE BRUTALIST DESIGN MEETS
WHOLESOME NATURE

MARZAHN,
BERLIN

▷⋯ STARTING POINT	⋯✕ DESTINATION
AHRENSFELDE S-BAHN STATION	**SCHLOSSPLATZBRAUEREI KÖPENICK**
🍺 BEER NAME	🎲 DIFFICULTY
HELLES	**HARD**
🚃 TRANSPORT	🕐 DURATION
S7, RB25	**4 H 30 MIN.**
⛰ ZONE	↦ LENGTH
B	**19 KM**
🔍 HIGHLIGHTS	〰 ELEVATION GAIN
EICHEPARK, GÄRTEN DER WELT, STADION AN DER ALTEN FÖRSTEREI, ALTSTADT KÖPENICK	ASCENT: 80 M DESCENT: 110 M

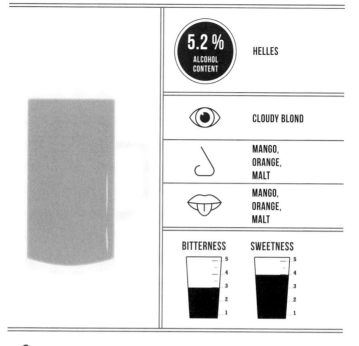

5.2 % ALCOHOL CONTENT		HELLES
		CLOUDY BLOND
		MANGO, ORANGE, MALT
		MANGO, ORANGE, MALT

BITTERNESS

SWEETNESS

HELLES. A rich and full-bodied fruity Helles that is both sweet and refreshing, with only a mild bitterness.

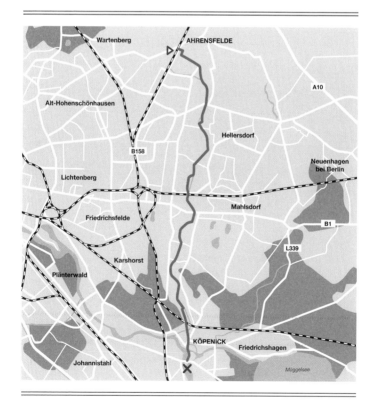

HIKE DESCRIPTION

The Wuhle River flows from north of Berlin down the city's border with Brandenburg all the way to the Köpenick district before joining the River Spree. The tributary's embankments are lined with protected green spaces that sit next to Soviet-era brutalist apartment complexes. Here in the outskirts of Berlin, you can find some of the city's finest natural spaces, teeming with wildlife, while the Wuhle winds its way through a series of hills that provide some very rewarding vantage points. Our walk also passes next to the public park known as Gärten der Welt (Gardens of the World), which adds yet another aspect to the unique beauty of this ecologically rich area.

Leaving the station, cross Märkische Allee and follow the blue #14 signposts, which will direct take you all the way to Köpenick. Turn right on Eichhorster Straße, then left on Havemannstraße, which you'll follow for a kilometer to arrive at Eichepark. Here, the Wuhletal-Wanderweg path is regularly signposted as it makes its way along the water.

Heading south along the Wuhletal-Wanderweg, you'll pass a field where highland cattle graze and soon reach the western summit of the Ahrensfelder Hills, the fourth highest point in Berlin at 114.5 meters. Crossing Landsberger Allee, the path leads further southward through fields overrun by wild hops.

After a kilometer, the path passes beneath the cable car that connects the Gärten der Welt to Kienberg Park. During the spring months, the area surrounding the Gärten der Welt turns into a hotspot for migrating geese, who hijack the stillness with their persistent honking. To the right, you'll see Kienberg Hill, from whose summit you can look out across the city.

As you continue to follow the signs, the path crosses the Wuhle after around 1.2 kilometers and then passes directly beneath the Wuhletal S-Bahn. Crossing the Wuhle once more immediately after leaving the station, the path heads south, passing through the idyllic district of Biesdorf, its garden homes filled with vegetables and colorful plants.

Two kilometers outside of Köpenick, a signpost pointing towards the Altstadt will take you across the stream once more and back into civilization on Mozartstraße, from which you'll turn left onto Hämmerlingstraße. Continue south on Hämmerlingstraße for 1.4 kilometers, under the train tracks and past the stadium of FC Union Berlin, one of the city's biggest football teams.

Turn left at Annenallee, right on Bahnhofstraße, and then left again at the junction with Lindenstraße, crossing the Dammbrücke and entering the historic center of Köpenick. Savor the medieval surroundings, replete with cobbled roads and centuries-old buildings.

Follow the Alt-Köpenick road into the town square, past the St. Laurentius church (originally built in the 14th century), the illustrious town hall, and numerous old-timey restaurants. The road eventually arrives at the Schlossplatz. This open and inviting square is right in front of the baroque Schloss Köpenick (Köpenick Palace), one of the most picturesque landmarks in the city. Here you'll find the Schlossplatzbrauerei Köpenick, often full of locals getting together to admire their fine surroundings and enjoy quality drinks.

SCHLOSSPLATZBRAUEREI KÖPENICK

Once deemed the smallest brewery in Germany, the Schlossplatzbrauerei is located on the regal Schlossplatz in Köpenick's historic town center. Although the team no longer make their beer on-site, the new brewery—now with increased capacity—has remained local. The cozy bar and accompanying terrace offer an exotic selection of beers, including a cherry-chili brew, as well as IPAs, Dunkels, and hoppy Lagers. The bar is a magnet for locals, who quickly fill the few seats squeezed between the bar and the old copper kettles. There is no food served, which means you can spend more energy focusing on the excellent beer menu.

ADDRESS

Schlossplatzbrauerei Köpenick
Grünstraße 24
12555 Berlin
+49 30 42096876
www.schlossplatzbrauerei-koepenick.de

Photos © Daniel Cole/Yvonne Hartmann

NORTH BERLIN

CHERRY BLOSSOM ROAD

A STROLL ALONG THE REUNIFICATION LINES

PANKOW, BRANDENBURG

▷··· STARTING POINT	···✕ DESTINATION
SCHÖNHOLZ S-BAHN STATION	BRÄUGIER BREWPUB
🍺 BEER NAME	🔢 DIFFICULTY
SUMMER IPA	MODERATE
🚃 TRANSPORT	🕐 DURATION
S1, S25, S26	1 H 30 MIN.
🗻 ZONE	↦ LENGTH
B	7.7 KM
🔍 HIGHLIGHTS	〰 ELEVATION GAIN
BERLIN WALL, CHERRY BLOSSOM ROAD (KIRSCHBLÜTENPFAD), MAUERPARK (WALL PARK)	ASCENT: 30 M DESCENT: 20 M

 SUMMER IPA

 LIGHT COPPER
WITH A CREAMY WHITE
HEAD

 MALTY,
CITRUS FRUITS

 HERBY,
ORANGE,
MALTS

BITTERNESS

SWEETNESS

 SUMMER IPA. A crisp and well-balanced tropical ale that is both
refreshing and big on taste.

HIKE DESCRIPTION

During the era of the Berlin Wall, the first checkpoint allowing citizens to cross the border was opened at Bornholmer Straße. It was one of the most significant moments in the history of Berlin, and it's been fittingly commemorated with a sea of cherry blossom trees along the old Wall route. This historical walk takes you along the path of the former Wall—bits and pieces of which are still visible—which today does no more than delimit the districts of Pankow and Wedding. Our route then brings you to the Prenzlauer Berg district, a former East Berlin neighborhood that has reaped the benefits of reunification.

Leaving the station, head north on Provinzstraße until you meet the signposted Berlin Wall Trail. Follow the trail south as it curves onto Am Bürgerpark, bordering the Pankow cemetery. Head south for 750 meters, turn right on Wilhelm-Kuhr-Straße, and follow the path that runs south parallel to the train tracks, an area interspersed with cherry trees.

Follow the Wall Trail south along Steegerstraße, doing a U-turn at the end of the road, crossing the park space in the middle of the road, and heading back on Grüntaler Straße. After passing under the train tracks, turn south on the Kirschblütenpfad footpath, which runs under the Bösebrücke at Bornholmer Straße. The Kirschblütenpfad footpath is lined on either side by Japanese cherry blossom trees and is full of visitors during the spring, when the trees bloom in their bright pink colors.

After Bösebrücke, the footpath turns into Norwegerstraße. Follow Norwegerstraße south, crossing over Behmstraße and onto and across the Schwedter Steg footbridge. At the end of the bridge on Schwedter Straße is a small footpath on your right that will take you onto an embankment with a footpath that leads on through small gardens and more cherry blossom trees. Head south along the embankment for 200 meters as it crosses Gleimstraße into Mauer Park. Head south directly through the park for 800 meters and arrive at Eberswalder Straße.

Leaving the park, cross Eberswalder Straße and head south on Oderberger Straße, taking note of one of the city's best craft-beer bars, Manifest Taproom. After crossing Schönhausser Allee, head east on Sredzkistraße, where you'll pass by the KulturBrauerei, the former Schultheiß brewery and now the location of the annual Beer Week Festival in September.

After 500 meters on Sredzkistraße, take a left at Kollwitzstraße and follow it northward. After 500 meters, turn right on Stubbenkammerstraße, and you'll arrive at the Bräugier Brewpub.

BRÄUGIER BREWPUB

The brewery and taprooms here are synonymous in Berlin with warm and welcoming good vibes. Established in 2017, Bräugier is a relatively new addition to the Berlin scene. Its reputation is built upon its creativity; the ever-changing menu always suggests something bold and new. Bräugier is especially well known for its rich and flavorful mix of IPAs. With twelve taps and a fridge stocked with beers from other local suppliers, nothing on offer will go begging here. The intimate and personable atmosphere has also helped make Bräugier a success. And although there's no food on-site, you're welcome to bring your own from any of the restaurants in the neighborhood.

ADDRESS

Bräugier BrewPub Prenzlauer Berg
Stubbenhammerstraße 6
10437 Berlin
+49 30 80098514
www.braeugier.de

Photos © Daniel Cole

HUMBOLDTHAIN

THE BEST VIEW OVER BERLIN

WEDDING,
BERLIN

▷⋯ STARTING POINT	⋯✕ DESTINATION
VOLTASTRASSE U-BAHN STATION	**VAGABUND BRAUEREI KESSELHAUS**
🍺 BEER NAME	🔢 DIFFICULTY
DAY PARTY	**EASY**
🚃 TRANSPORT	🕐 DURATION
U8	**1 H**
⛰ ZONE	↦ LENGTH
A	**4.7 KM**
🔍 HIGHLIGHTS	〰 ELEVATION GAIN
ROSE GARDEN HUMBOLDTHAIN, HUMBOLDTHAIN FLAK TOWERS, SILENT GREEN KULTURQUARTIER	ASCENT: 30 M DESCENT: 40 M

3.5 %
ALCOHOL
CONTENT

HAZY IPA

GOLDEN,
LIGHT

SWEET FRUITS

PINEAPPLE,
SLIGHT HOPS

BITTERNESS	SWEETNESS
5	5
4	4
3	3
2	2
1	1

DAY PARTY. This breezy, subtle ale is rich with fruity tastes that add
character without overwhelming the balance or composure of the beer.

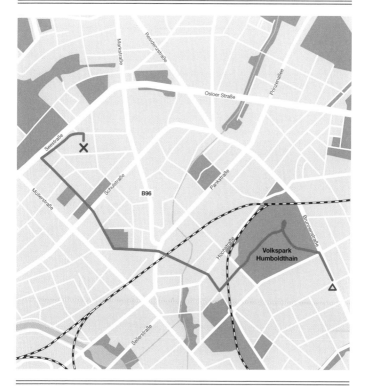

HIKE DESCRIPTION

Climbing the old anti-aircraft flak tower in Volkspark Humboldthain rewards you with some of the most gratifying views the city has to offer. Although the facility was partly destroyed after the Second World War, two towers remain next to the park's rose gardens. The giant concrete ramparts are now lined with trees and have become more park fixtures than war turrets. They're just a few of many fantastic features of the park—which is named for the Prussian explorer Alexander von Humboldt. Other highlights include a swimming pool, a vineyard, and a water park.

Leaving the station, head north on Brunnenstraße, cross Gustav-Meyer-Allee, and enter the Volkspark Humboldthain. Take the first left and head northwest into the center of the park. After 200 meters, at the commemorative statue to Humboldt, take a right and proceed to the enclosed rose gardens. At the gates to the garden, a set of stairs leads upward to your left. Make your way up the stairs toward the embankments of the turret, stopping to look out across the city at the very top of stairway.

Take the stairs back down and at the very bottom, next to the rose garden, turn right and follow the pathway for 800 meters until you've exited the park. Once out of the park, cross Wiesenstraße and proceed down Grenzstraße. After 500 meters, take a right on Gerichtstraße.

Walk down Gerichtstraße for a kilometer. After crossing Nettelbeck-platz, you'll come to the Silent Green Kulturquartier, a luscious new garden and event space on the grounds of a former crematorium. Directly afterward, turn right on Ruheplatzstraße and follow it north for one kilometer. Ruheplatzstraße turns into Turiner Straße and passes through Leopoldplatz.

At Seestraße, turn right and proceed for 400 meters; then turn right again onto Oudenarder Straße. Soon you'll come to the Osram-Höfe courtyard, where a former factory is home to the Vagabund brewing team.

VAGABUND BRAUEREI KESSELHAUS

Located in the premises of a huge former lightbulb factory, Vagabund's new brewery and bar have an easy and carefree feel thanks to the expansive outdoor area and post-industrial aesthetic. Originally established by a trio of Americans looking to reshape the city's beer scene, the new Kesselhaus has a wealth of beers on offer, all rooted in a desire for creativity and variety, with pales and IPAs leading the way. The secluded brewery is a real treasure trove for those who can find it, and although there's no fixed menu, there are occasional vendors who set up shop in the courtyard to feed hungry beer-wanderers a mixed assortment of international victuals.

ADDRESS

Vagabund Brauerei Kesselhaus
Oudenarder Straße 16–20
13347 Berlin
+49 33 17043211
www.vagabundbrauerei.com

Photos © Yvonne Hartmann

TEGELER FLIESS

STREAMS AND FARMS: ALONG THE BERLIN WALL

REINICKENDORF, BERLIN

▷┄ STARTING POINT	┄✕ DESTINATION
WAIDMANNSLUST S-BAHN STATION	**TWO FELLAS BREWERY**
🍺 BEER NAME	🎛 DIFFICULTY
CALIFORNIA COMMON	**HARD**
🚆 TRANSPORT	🕐 DURATION
S1, S2, S26	**4 H**
⛰ ZONE	↦ LENGTH
B	**16 KM**
🔍 HIGHLIGHTS	〰 ELEVATION GAIN
TEGELER FLIESS, LÜBARS VILLAGE CHURCH, BERLIN WALL ROUTE	ASCENT: 70 M DESCENT: 30 M

| 4.5 % ALCOHOL CONTENT | PILSNER |

| LIGHT GOLDEN |

| CITRUSY, HERB |

| CLEAN, MALTY, SLIGHT FRUIT |

| BITTERNESS | SWEETNESS |

CALIFORNIA COMMON. A fresh, herby pilsner with undertones of malt and summer fruits, enriched with a healthy dose of Californian summer goodness.

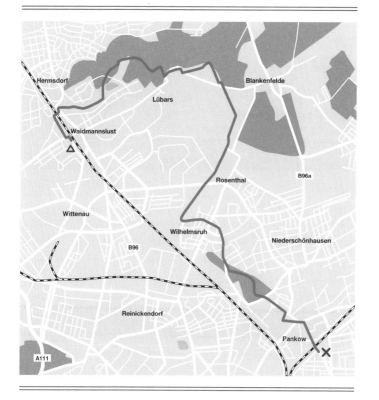

HIKE DESCRIPTION

Along the city's northern border, a wildlife reserve beside a creek connects several large lakes and marshlands. It's an area isolated from the big city, full of natural beauty, wildflower fields, and picturesque farmland. This walk connects two great hiking trails: the Barnimer Dörferweg and the Berliner Mauerweg, the latter of which follows the path of the former Berlin Wall. At the heart of the area is pristinely preserved Lübars, the oldest village in Berlin. This centuries-old hamlet is surrounded by traditional farms, and you're sure to see a lot of people riding horses. Amid the cobbled streets sits a church as old as Berlin itself, with a fine baroque interior. Following the old trail into Pankow, our walk passes through two of the city's northernmost parks—Volkspark Schönholzer Heide and Bürgerpark Pankow—before eventually arriving at the Two Fellas Brewery, a modern bar founded by a couple of beer-loving expats that illustrates the city's international spirit.

Immediately upon leaving the station, head east on Waidmannsluster Damm and then turn directly north on Artemisstraße. After 500 meters, you'll reach the Tegeler Fließ, a creek that runs for 8 kilometers through the northern part of the city into the Tegeler See. Follow the creekside walkway eastward for the next 5 kilometers.

The route you're following is the signposted Barnimer Dörferweg, one of the city's best walking routes. After crossing Berliner Straße, you'll pass the Hermsdorfer See, a beautiful expanse of water lined with reeds and home to a variety of birds and ducks.

The path carries on past a public swimming pool before reaching a junction where several walkways intersect. Seven hundred meters after Hermsdorfer See, at the next junction, the path to the left turns

into a series of walkways that cross a protected marshland teeming with wildlife. The route that we'll take, however, is still signposted "Barnimer Dörferweg" and leads into a field rich with rare and colorful wildflowers. As the path curves, you'll start to see the farms of the village of Lübars appearing in the distance.

Keep to the signposted route and take a left up a mild incline toward the village. On every side, you'll see rustic farmhouses and many horses. After 1.5 kilometers, on reaching street level, follow the signs into the center of the village, where you'll come upon the village church.

From the church, follow Alt-Lübars, passing a herb farm on the corner, and continue until the cobbled road ends. Here you'll see a signposted country path on your left. Follow it for 900 meters through more fields

of idyllic wildflowers until you reach the next iconic walking path, the Berliner Mauerweg. As you follow the Berliner Mauerweg south for the next 3 kilometers, you'll be rewarded with excellent views of the city center and surrounding areas. After a while, the path starts to follow a disused railway line that once connected Berlin to the village of Wandlitz.

After walking beside the tracks for a few kilometers, you'll see civilization start to reemerge as the Mauerweg weaves its way into the city suburbs. As you enter the Alt-Rosenthal district, more remnants of the abandoned railway will emerge, with old signal lights and station signs visible from the road. Cross Quickborner Straße and continue to follow the Mauerweg for 400 meters until you reach Wilhelmsruher Damm. Here, you'll leave the Mauerweg to carry on along Uhlandstraße. After a kilometer, you'll reach Lessingstraße in the district of Wilhelmsruh.

Take a left on Lessingstraße and head east for 500 meters; then take a right on Schönholzer Weg and follow it for a kilometer. Directly in front of you will be the Volkspark Schönholzer Heide, home to one of the city's Soviet memorials. As you head into the park, take the path on the left that leads directly southward, parallel to Friesenstraße. After 500 meters, you'll reach a junction from which you can head right into the park's center, through the teeming wilderness, and out again onto Heinrich-Mann-Straße. Follow Heinrich-Mann-Straße for a kilometer into the heart of Pankow. On the right, you'll see Bürgerpark Pankow, which is worth detouring through to see the immaculately kept gardens, rose bushes, and water features.

At the end of Heinrich-Mann-Straße, cross the Panke and follow Schönholzer Straße and then Breite Straße, passing the impressive red-brick town hall. Then head directly south on Mühlenstraße until you reach the welcoming arms of Two Fellas, where a glass of summer Pilsner awaits you in the brewery's neighborly garden.

TWO FELLAS BREWERY

This modern brewery was established in 2017 by two Americans, Mike Moineau and Rob Faber. The taps are supplied with well-curated, Berlin-brewed IPAs and Pilsners, in addition to Two Fellas's own lagers and IPAs. When you step into the bar, the brewery room is immediately visible. The Two Fellas team is a veritable mix of locals and expats, highlighting the bar's multicultural atmosphere, which mixes classic American hospitality with German traditions. Enjoy the great beer garden and the American meals available on the weekends—among them Two Fellas's famed Chicago deep-pan pizzas.

ADDRESS

Two Fellas Brewery
Mühlenstraße 30
13187 Berlin
+49 176 61375525
drink@twofellas.beer
www.twofellas.beer

Photos © Lisa Khanna

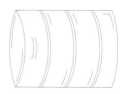

TEGEL

THE HOME OF THE TRUE BERLINER WEISSE

CHARLOTTENBURG, BERLIN

▷··· STARTING POINT	···✕ DESTINATION
HALEMWEG U-BAHN STATION	**SCHNEEEULE**
🍺 BEER NAME	🎲 DIFFICULTY
MARLENE	**MODERATE**
🚌 TRANSPORT	🕐 DURATION
U7	**2 H**
⛰ ZONE	↦ LENGTH
B	**9.2 KM**
👁 HIGHLIGHTS	〰 ELEVATION GAIN
JUNGFERNHEIDE VOLKSPARK, TEGEL AIRPORT, BERLIN-SPANDAU SHIP CANAL	ASCENT: 20 M DESCENT: 20 M

BERLINER WEISSE

CLOUDY YELLOW

**MUSTY, SOUR,
FRUITS, FLOWERY**

**SOUR,
GRAPEFRUIT**

BITTERNESS

5
4
3
2
1

SWEETNESS

5
4
3
2
1

MARLENE. Like its namesake, Marlene Dietrich, this thirst-quenching sour is a Berlin classic. With complex floral and grapefruit notes, this beer has a texture reminiscent of wine.

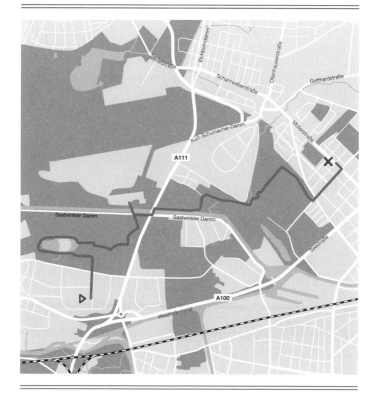

HIKE DESCRIPTION

Tegel was once Berlin's main airport, and its modernist design was the envy of the world. When the new Berlin Brandenburg Airport opened in 2020, however, Tegel closed its doors. Located in northern Berlin, Tegel sits just to the north of Jungfernheide Park, a former hunting grounds featuring open green spaces, wildlife, and even a public beach. To the east of the airport is the stunning Rehberge Park, where there are several lakes, animal reserves, and an open-air cinema. Along with the shipping canal, now a plaything for the luxury boating community, the area displays an interesting contrast of landscapes in which wild nature is juxtaposed with the industrial relics of a bygone era.

Leaving the station, head north on Halemweg into the Jungfernheide Volkspark. Follow the path leading northward into the park and, after about 300 meters, take your second left. Turn right at the end of the path, in front of the Jungfernheide Biergarten, and then turn left and follow the lakeside path in a clockwise direction before eventually circling around the public beach. As you head back into the center of the park, following the water's edge, make your way toward the Water Tower that looks out across the park.

Round the Water Tower counterclockwise and walk to the eastern edge of the park. Turn left and follow the park path that runs parallel to the A111 highway until you reach the junction with Saatwinkler Damm, from where you can peer across the General-Ganeval-Brücke into the former airport. Head east on Saatwinkler Damm for 300 meters. On the south side of the road, just under Hinckeldeybrücke, are a set of stairs that will take you to a public footpath that carries on on the other side of the canal.

Once you've crossed the bridge, descend to the canal and follow it eastward. After a few hundred meters, the path passes a set of luxurious allotments where local Berliners have built summer retreats with elaborate gardens and an abundance of flags.

After 2 kilometers following the path along the allotments, you'll arrive in Rehberge Public Park. Take the first left and head north, where after 750 meters, you'll arrive at an age-old open-air cinema. Take the path that heads southeast along the Möwensee and follow it until it exits the park at Transvaalstraße. Turn left and follow Transvaalstraße northeast for 800 meters to reach Müllerstraße. Turn left on Müllerstraße and then take the first right to arrive at the doors of the Schneeeule Salon.

SCHNEEEULE SALON FÜR BERLINER BIERKULTUR

Only Weiße made in Berlin can be called Berliner Weiße, and the best varieties are be found in brewmaster Ulrike Genz's cozy salon. Bringing back the city's historical beer in its classical style, Schneeeule offers a variety of Weißes with differing aged and aromatic flavors. These light sour beers, once referred to as "the champagne of the north" (Ulrike even has a champagne Weiße on the menu), are not just integral to Berlin's history, but are wholesomely refreshing with their multitude of complex flavors. The salon-bar has a complete selection of all Schneeeule's brews, with additional guest-beers also available on tap. The rustic-style bar also offers regular tasting sessions and games nights, and although there's no food menu, there's plenty of international cuisine on offer in the neighborhood.

ADDRESS

Schneeeule Salon für Berliner Bierkultur
Ofener Straße 1
13349
Berlin
+49 30 98437323
www.schneeeule.berlin

Photos © Yvonne Hartmann

MOABIT

FROM THE CITY CENTER TO THE SEA OF PLEASURE: PLÖTZENSEE AND BEYOND

MOABIT, BERLIN

▷⋯ STARTING POINT	⋯✕ DESTINATION
HAUPTBAHNHOF	**ESCHENBRÄU**
🍺 BEER NAME	🁢 DIFFICULTY
PANKE GOLD	**EASY**
🚃 TRANSPORT	🕓 DURATION
U5, S-BAHN, REGIONAL SERVICES	**1 H 15 MIN.**
⌂ ZONE	↦ LENGTH
A	**7 KM**
🔍 HIGHLIGHTS	〰 ELEVATION GAIN
HAUPTBAHNHOF, KRAFTWERK MOABIT, PLÖTZENSEE	ASCENT: 20 M DESCENT: 20 M

5.1 %
ALCOHOL
CONTENT

PALE ALE

HAZY PALE GOLD

CITRUS,
FLOWERS

PINEAPPLE,
GRAIN,
GRAPEFRUIT

BITTERNESS	SWEETNESS

 PANKE GOLD. A one-of-a-kind, medium-bodied, dry-hopped, freshly poured aromatic lager that is rich in fruity citrus and floral flavors.

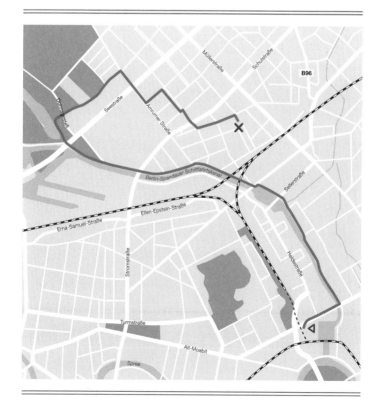

HIKE DESCRIPTION

Berlin Central Station might not seem the likeliest place to start a hike, but its location next to the scenic Berlin-Spandau Ship Canal offers a great starting point for a waterside adventure. This route takes you along the former Berlin Wall to Plötzensee, a beautiful city lake and a great place for wasting away never-ending summer days, before arriving in the northern district of Wedding.

Leaving the bustle of the Hauptbahnhof on Invalidenstraße, head east past the Hamburger Bahnhof—an immaculately preserved 19th-century train station, now a contemporary art space—and cross over the Mauerweg Brücke. Once over the bridge, you'll find the Berlin Wall Trail on your left. Follow the cobbled road north along the canal as it enters the Invalids' Cemetery, which, besides being home to the graves of military servicemen, is the final resting ground of many who died attempting to cross the Berlin Wall. On leaving the cemetery through its northern entrance, you'll pass the Günter Litfin Memorial, an old guard tower now dedicated to the first person killed attempting to flee to West Berlin.

After passing through the grassy Nordhafen, where the Panke (the river our featured beer takes its name from) feeds into the canal, the walkway crosses Fennstraße into the leafy district of Moabit. Follow the canal path for 2 kilometers and cross Seestraße, where the idyllic blue waters of the Plötzensee will beckon you onward, inviting you to rent a boat or chill on the beach.

Follow the edge of the Plötzensee round to the east for 200 meters and take the second woodland path on the right. Cross Dohnagestell, walk through Goethepark, and arrive at Afrikanische Straße. Turn right on Afrikanische Straße, cross over Seestraße, and continue on Amrumer

Straße. Turn left onto Brüsseler Straße. Head up Brüsseler Straße, passing the Anti-War Museum; then turn right on Lütticher Straße and proceed to its end. Walk through the carpark, cross Luxemburger Straße, and continue for 50 meters to Triftstraße. Head east on Triftstraße for 200 meters until you reach Genter Straße, where Eschenbräu can be found tucked away inside the estate on your left.

ESCHENBRÄU

This somewhat hidden neighborhood brewery is a northern German facsimile of what you would typically find in Franconia, with a large outdoor seating area, delightful beers, and community spirit. The brainchild of local brewmaster Martin Eschenbräu, the beer garden and bar are located in the courtyard of a student residence where Martin himself used to live. Here you can sample fresh craft beers year-round—Pilsners, Dunkels, and Weizens—along with some seasonal delights. You can also try some of Martin's other concoctions, such as schnapps and whiskies. The bar also offers *Flammkuchen*, aka tarts, delivered directly to your table with an amiable courtesy you'll only find here in Eschenbräu's secret corner.

ADDRESS

Eschenbräu
Triftstraße 67
13353 Berlin
+49 162 4931915
info@eschenbraeu.de
www.eschenbraeu.de

Photos © Yvonne Hartmann

PANKE ROAD

ALONG ONE OF BERLIN'S GREEN WALKS
TO A REMOTE BEER COMMUNITY

PANKOW, BERLIN

▷⋯ STARTING POINT	⋯✕ DESTINATION
BUCH S-BAHN STATION	**ERSTE BERNAUER BRAUGENOSSENSCHAFT**
🍺 BEER NAME	DIFFICULTY
DAS BERNAUER	**MODERATE**
🚃 TRANSPORT	⏱ DURATION
S2	**3 H 15 MIN.**
⛰ ZONE	↦ LENGTH
B	**14 KM (ONE WAY)**
🔎 HIGHLIGHTS	〰 ELEVATION GAIN
SCHLOSSPARK BUCH, PANKE, BERNAU, BÖRNICKE CHILDREN'S FARM	ASCENT: 50 M DESCENT: 20 M

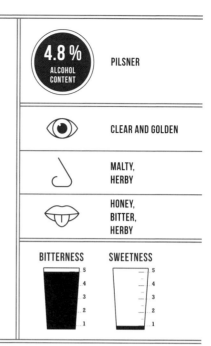

4.8% ALCOHOL CONTENT	PILSNER
(eye)	CLEAR AND GOLDEN
(nose)	MALTY, HERBY
(mouth)	HONEY, BITTER, HERBY

BITTERNESS
5
4
3
2
1

SWEETNESS
5
4
3
2
1

DAS BERNAUER. A light and bitter North-German pilsner that features subtle notes of fruit and honey and goes down smooth.

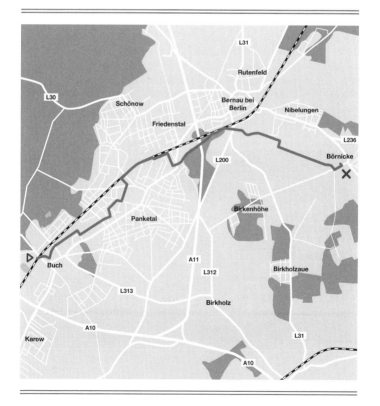

HIKE DESCRIPTION

The Panke, Berlin's third-largest river, winds its way out of the city toward the historic village of Bernau. One of Berlin's best walks leads along the Panke through long, pristine fields and nature reserves, taking you out of Berlin and through secluded villages into lush, green farmland, where a local collective has set up a new brewery dedicated to traditional beer-making methods.

For most of this hike, the route follows the Pankeweg hiking trail, which in Berlin is marked by blue signs with the number 5 on them. Outside of Berlin, the route is marked by a red square. The path is also used by cyclists. It is well signposted, with frequent signs directing you toward Bernau.

Leaving the station, cross Wiltbergstraße and head directly north into Schlosspark Buch, following the blue signposts. At the north side of the park, cross Pölnitzweg and follow the Panke north to the village of Panketal.

In Panketal, turn left on Bahnhofstraße and then immediately right on Triftstraße, which you'll follow for 800 meters. Turn right on Straße der Jugend and then follow the signposts north through fields that are often full of horses. Cross Schönerlinder Straße, head north on Post-straße, and then turn left immediately on Eisenbahnstraße.

At the end of Eisenbahnstraße turn right and follow the footpath next to the rail tracks north for 2 kilometers, crossing the Panke once again. Continue along Ernst-Moritz-Arndt-Straße and then turn right on Eichendorffstraße and follow it southward for 400 meters. Turn left on Theodor-Körner-Straße, cross Zepernicker Chaussee, and take the countryside path that follows the Panke once more for 2.5 kilometers.

Crossing beneath the motorway and passing a fishing lake, you'll arrive at Weißenseer Straße. Follow the signposts to Bernau, turning right, crossing Weißenseer Straße, and heading north on Hesselweg.

After 300 meters, a right turn will lead you through an ostrich farm. After the ostrich farm, take the first left and follow it through the fields along a stream. After 500 meters, turn right and cross the stream. Immediately after crossing the stream, follow the unnamed path that separates the town from the field counterclockwise to your right. After one kilometer, with the field always on your right, you'll meet the Jakobsweg, which cuts through acres of farmyards and fields and is marked with yellow-squared signs. Follow the Jakobsweg for two kilometers, first southward and then veering to the east.

Pass through the Börnicke Children's farm, filled with highland cattle, geese, and pigs, and then take a left on Ernst-Thälmann-Straße, where the Bernauer Braugenossenschaft beckons you after a couple minutes' walk. To return, there are bus services to Bernau and to Werneuchen, from either of which connecting trains will take you to Berlin.

ERSTE BERNAUER BRAUGENOSSENSCHAFT

The medieval town of Bernau was once home to a proud brewing tradition, that has been lost as the centuries passed. In 2016, however, a bunch of beer-loving locals got together to form a collective dedicated to making traditional Bernau beer to modern standards. In 2020, the collective founded its own brewery in an old distillery in the village of Börnicke, just outside of Bernau. The old factory and farmhouse setting makes for an idyllic countryside location. Occasionally, fresh barbequed foods and pub fare are cooked on the terrace, but you can always find Pilsner, Dunkel, and pale ales being poured on-site, with a regularly rotating seasonal beer also available.

ADDRESS

Erste Bernauer Braugenossenschaft eG.
Ernst-Thälmann-Straße 2c
16321 Bernau bei Berlin
+49 33 38768528
post@braugenosse.de
www.braugenosse.de

Photos © Yvonne Hartmann

WEST BERLIN

ANHALTER BAHNHOF

THE PARK OF FORGOTTEN TRAIN LINES

MITTE, BERLIN

▷··· STARTING POINT	···✗ DESTINATION
HAUSVOGTEIPLATZ U-BAHN STATION	**BRLO BRWHOUSE**
🍺 BEER NAME	🀫 DIFFICULTY
BRLO PALE ALE	**EASY**
🚃 TRANSPORT	🕐 DURATION
U2	**1 H**
⛰ ZONE	↦ LENGTH
A	**5 KM**
🔎 HIGHLIGHTS	⌁ ELEVATION GAIN
FRANZÖSISCHER DOM/GENDARMENMARKT, CHECKPOINT CHARLIE, ANHALTER BAHNHOF,	ASCENT: 10 M DESCENT: 0 M

6.0 % ALCOHOL CONTENT — PALE ALE

GOLDEN, CLOUDY AMBER

GRAPEFRUIT, MANGO

CARAMEL, HOPS, BERRIES

BITTERNESS

SWEETNESS

BRLO PALE ALE. A fruity and hoppy ale that triggers a multitude of taste receptors; this brew has an aftertaste of mango and mildly bitter citrus.

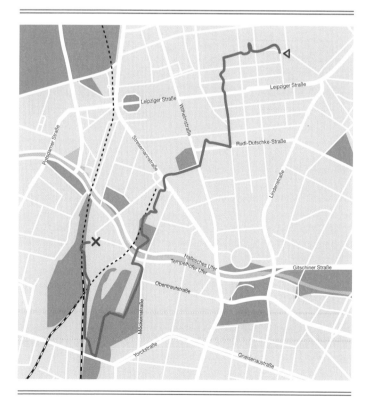

HIKE DESCRIPTION

From the baroque royal square of Gendarmenmarkt, across Berlin's most famed wall-crossing point—Checkpoint Charlie—through the abandoned railway lines in Gleisdreieck, and to the vibrant, modern settings of BRLO, this hike shows that Berlin really has it all. The exposed and ruined facade of the Anhalter Bahnhof speaks of a history of postindustrial decline in which both the destruction caused by Allied bombing and the erection of the Berlin Wall led to the downfall of many international rail lines serving Berlin. When the Wall came down, most of the nearby land was reclaimed for the public in the form of Gleisdreieck Park, where the brewery, bar, and restaurant BRLO is now found.

Starting at Hausvogteiplatz, head west on Taubenstraße, cross Markgrafenstraße and enter straight into Gendarmenmarkt, one of the most beautiful and historic squares in Berlin, surrounded by the Französischer Dom and Deutscher Dom churches and the Berlin Concert House.

Cross Charlottenstraße on the other side of the square and continue west on Taubenstraße for a block until you reach the partially pedestrianized Friedrichstraße. Head south on Friedrichstraße until Checkpoint Charlie, which is distinguished by the historic pictures of American and Soviet soldiers looking across the old border station. After you've had your picture taken here, head further south for another block and turn right on Kochstraße, then left at the junction with Wilhelmstraße and right again on Anhalter Straße.

As soon as you turn onto Anhalter Straße, the facade of the old Anhalter Bahnhof looms ahead. Walk to the right of the sports pitch directly toward Tempodrom and then take the path to the right, following it around and through Elise-Tilse-Park, where the remnants of the station's platforms are still visible.

At the end of the park on Hallesches Ufer take Anhalter Steg, a pedestrian footbridge that crosses the Landwehr Canal. On the other side of the canal, follow the footpath directly ahead into Park am Gleisdreieck, continuing along the still-visible railway tracks. Head in a straight line through the park for 900 meters. When the park ends at Yorckstraße, head right for 100 meters and then turn right again and follow the park path north for a kilometer, walking parallel to the intercity railway lines. Pass the skatepark and graffiti wall, walk beneath the U-Bahn bridge that crosses the entire park, and you'll find yourself directly at BRLO's beer garden.

BRLO BRWHOUSE

Much more than a brewhouse and restaurant, BRLO Brwhouse (not a typo!) is a modern Berlin institution. Progressive, inclusive, environmentally friendly, and regularly involved in local community initiatives, BRLO represents what modern Berlin stands for. ("Brlo" is the original Old Slavic name for Berlin.) Eating in the restaurant is a fine dining experience, with predominantly vegetarian haute cuisine in an elaborately lit setting. Outdoors, the extensive beer garden offers viewings of major sports events. The organic brewery now operates to carbon-neutral standards. New varieties of beer pop up regularly, as do guest collaborations with local and international breweries—and even famous rap stars such as Run the Jewels—who have made several beers with BRLO.

ADDRESS

BRLO BRWHOUSE
Schöneberger Straße 16
10963 Berlin
+49 33 17043211
www.en.brlo.de/house-of-brewing

Photos © Yvonne Hartmann

SCHLOSS CHARLOTTENBURG

BERLIN'S ROYAL GARDENS

CHARLOTTENBURG, BERLIN

▷⋯ STARTING POINT	⋯✗ DESTINATION
JUNGFERNHEIDE U-BAHN STATION	**LEMKE AM SCHLOSS**
🍺 BEER NAME	🔢 DIFFICULTY
LEMKE WEIZEN	**EASY**
🚆 TRANSPORT	🕐 DURATION
U7, S41, S42, S46	**1 H**
⛰ ZONE	↦ LENGTH
A	**4.5 KM**
🔍 HIGHLIGHTS	〰 ELEVATION GAIN
BELVEDERE TEA HOUSE, MAUSOLEUM, SCHLOSS CHARLOTTENBURG	ASCENT: 10 M DESCENT: 0 M

5.5 % ALCOHOL CONTENT	HEFEWEIZEN
👁	CLOUDY DARK AMBER
👃	BANANA, VANILLA
👅	BANANA, APRICOT, CARAMEL

BITTERNESS	SWEETNESS
2 (of 5)	2 (of 5)

LEMKE WEIZEN. Looks incredible, and tastes even better. The thick and aromatic wheat beat explodes with sweet tastes that manifest in notes of banana, clove, and caramel on the tongue.

HIKE DESCRIPTION

Berlin's very own Versailles, Charlottenburg Palace and its royal gardens are some of the most picturesque and sublime sights you'll find in the entire city. Throughout the baroque gardens you'll discover rococo architecture, exotic plants, and a welcome serenity. Over 300 years old, the palace and grounds were once home to the Prussian queen Sophie Charlotte of Hanover, who famously practiced music here with an international cohort of guests. The palace was passed down along the Prussian royal line, with each king adding his own touch and flare to the ever-evolving residence.

Head west as you leave the station and follow the signposts across the Spree and into the palatial gardens. From here, you can easily lose yourself in the maze of pathways running between fields, streams, and floral landscapes. Head directly south from the park entrance for 300 meters and arrive at the Belvedere tea house, built in 1788.

As you follow the path around the Belvedere heading west, you'll be rewarded with a sterling view of the palace from behind the picturesque Hohe Brücke.

Following the Fürstenbrunner Graben stream around the park will allow you to take in the exotic plants and birds that inhabit the grounds. After following the stream for a kilometer to the west and then rounding the southern edge of the park, the path brings you to the Mausoleum and then to the colorful and well-preserved French gardens. A small bridge will then take you north over to the serene Luiseninsel in the middle of the carp pond, from which you'll see even more impressive views of the palace grounds. Head around the island, crossing the Hohe Brücke, and then head south directly through the gardens toward the palace.

Directly in front of the palace, turn left and head east toward the Schlossbrücke, passing the Neapolitan New Pavilion. Then cross Luisenplatz to the immaculate Lemke brewery.

LEMKE AM SCHLOSS

Established in a preexisting brewhouse built in the 1980s, Lemke moved into the Charlottenburg property in 2007 with the goal of carrying on the district's brewing legacy. Ironically enough, the brewhouse —Luisenbräu—was where Oli Lemke, founder of the Lemke Brewery, once worked while at university. Today, as one of three Lemke outlets (there are two more in Berlin), Lemke am Schloss brings a traditional and hearty vibe to its brewing. Here you'll find nourishing German cuisine as well as an impressive selection of beers, ranging from classics—Pilsners, Dunkels, etc.—to more adventurous offerings, such as those in the barrel-aged series. Whatever you choose, you'll struggle to get a bad drink here.

ADDRESS

Lemke am Schloss
Luisenplatz 1
10585 Berlin
+49 30 30878979
schloss@lemkeberlin.com
www.schloss.lemke.berlin

Photos © Yvonne Hartmann

SPANDAUER FOREST

RIVERSIDES, WOODLANDS & SWAMPS

SPANDAU, BERLIN

▷··· STARTING POINT	···✕ DESTINATION
HENNIGSDORF S-BAHN STATION	**BRAUHAUS SPANDAU**
🍺 BEER NAME	🎲 DIFFICULTY
SPANDAUER HAVELBRÄU	**HARD**
🚆 TRANSPORT	🕐 DURATION
S25	**4 H**
⛰ ZONE	↦ LENGTH
C	**15 KM**
🔍 HIGHLIGHTS	〰 ELEVATION GAIN
BORDER TOWER NIEDER NEUENDORF, SPANDAU WILDLIFE RESERVE TEUFELSBRUCH	ASCENT: 30 M DESCENT: 30 M

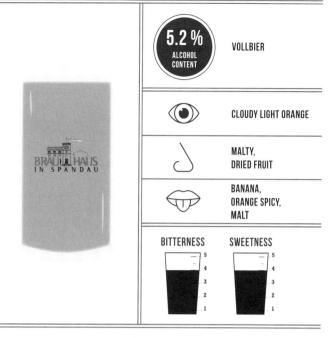

5.2 % ALCOHOL CONTENT — VOLLBIER

CLOUDY LIGHT ORANGE

MALTY,
DRIED FRUIT

BANANA,
ORANGE SPICY,
MALT

BITTERNESS — 5 4 3 2 1

SWEETNESS — 5 4 3 2 1

 SPANDAUER HAVELBRÄU. An unfiltered and refreshing spicy malt beer with delicious fruity notes that sit on your tongue long after you've guzzled it.

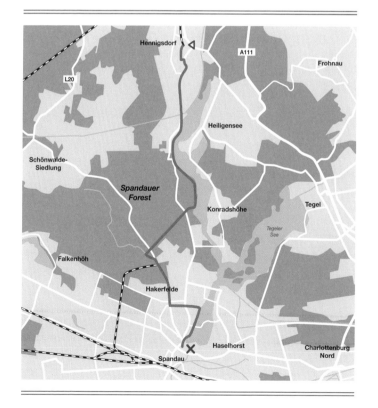

HIKE DESCRIPTION

Savor the stillness on this riverside walk on the outskirts of Berlin. As you stroll along the romantic Havel River, tranquil village surroundings are succeeded by verdant woods and wild swamplands. The initial section follows the Berlin Wall, which once separated the village of Hennigsdorf from the rest of the city, and many relics and historic monuments are on display to remind you that this peaceful area was once beset by division and hostility.

Leaving the station, head south on Rathernaustraße. Pass Am Rathenaupark and turn right on Spandauer Allee, which you'll follow for two kilometers, passing Waldpark. After crossing the Bridge of German–Soviet Friendship, take an immediate left onto the pedestrian path running parallel to the Havel River, which you'll follow south all the way into Berlin.

The riverside path doubles as the Berlin Wall Trail and passes by an old border watchtower after a kilometer. Six kilometers outside of Hennigsdorf, the path crosses the border into Berlin, entering a lush, open pine woodland before arriving at the restaurant Jagdhaus Spandau on the forest beach. Follow the signposted trail around the back of the restaurant, leave the Berlin Wall Trail, and follow the first road to the right for around 50 meters until you hit Niederneuendorfer Allee.

Cross Niederneuendorfer Allee and follow the woodland path directly into the woods. After 700 meters, the forest floor gives way to a wooden footpath leading across a temperate swampland filled with barren vegetation, frogs, and snakes.

Proceed for another 1.2 kilometers into the woods, cross Schönwalder Allee, and take a left after the Kuhlake stream. Pass directly through the nature reserve and, after 700 meters, turn east crossing the Kuhlake again, passing the wild boar enclosures and arriving back on Schönwalder Allee. Head south on Schönwalder Allee for 1.8 kilometers (Schönwalder Allee will turn into Fehrbelliner Tor after crossing Hohenzollernring) and then head east on Askanierring for 1.1 kilometers, crossing Streitstraße and continuing on Havelschanze until you reach the Havel River once again. Proceed southward on the footpath for 1.5 kilometers, following the river through an opulent suburban neighborhood and crossing Eiswerderstraße and Triftstraße to arrive at Wröhmännerstraße. Proceed on Wröhmännerstraße into Wröhmännerpark, the site of Brauhaus Spandau.

BRAUHAUS SPANDAU

Located in a renovated two-story red-brick building just outside of Spandau's old town, this traditionally styled brewhouse and restaurant is a shining crown of the city's beer scene and well worth the journey from central Berlin. Founded in 1994, the restaurant and bar surround the brewing kettles and there is a sizable outdoor terrace. Besides its Havelbräu, the brewery specializes in regularly rotating seasonal beers; its Märzen and Maibock are especially popular. The kitchen serves up excellent classics including Schweinshaxe, schnitzel, and a variety of sausage-based dishes. It's a full-on dining experience and very popular with the locals, so it's best to reserve ahead. You can also take a tour of the brewery, and take-away options are always available.

ADDRESS

Brauhaus Spandau
Neuendorfer Straße 1
13585 Berlin
+49 30 3539070
info@brauhaus-spandau.de
www.brauhaus-spandau.de

Photos © Yvonne Hartmann

TEGELER FOREST

FROM HEILIGENSEE TO TEGEL:
BERLIN'S BEAUTIFUL WEST

TEGEL, BERLIN

▷⋯ STARTING POINT	⋯✕ DESTINATION
HEILIGENSEE S-BAHN STATION	**KUBI'S POINT**
🍾 BEER NAME	🔡 DIFFICULTY
MESSING	**MODERATE**
🚃 TRANSPORT	🕐 DURATION
S25	**3 H 30 MIN.**
⛰ ZONE	↦ LENGTH
B	**13.7 KM**
🔎 HIGHLIGHTS	〰 ELEVATION GAIN
HEILIGENSEE, BURGSDORF LARCH, DICKE MARIE, THE ARCHAIC ARCHANGEL OF HEILIGENSEE, GREENWICH PROMENADE	ASCENT: 30 M DESCENT: 30 M

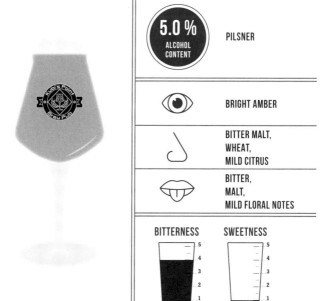

5.0 % ALCOHOL CONTENT	**PILSNER**
	BRIGHT AMBER
	BITTER MALT, WHEAT, MILD CITRUS
	BITTER, MALT, MILD FLORAL NOTES

BITTERNESS	SWEETNESS
5 4 3 2 1	5 4 3 2 1

MESSING. A very light, slightly sweet, and decidedly bitter crystal-clear pilsner with a subtle herbal and floral aftertaste.

HIKE DESCRIPTION

Within the wild pine woodlands of Tegeler Forst are many hidden surprises. Here you'll not only discover Berlin's tallest tree, but also its oldest, the 900-year-old oak known as Dicke Marie. There are desert-like dunes, a wild-animal reserve, and the odd palace here and there, all tucked away between the Greenwich Promenade and the picturesque village of Heiligensee.

Leaving the station, head north briefly on Ruppiner Chaussee before taking a left on Hennigsdorfer Straße, which runs parallel to the Havel River. After 800 meters, turn left on Kurzebracker Weg. After about 50 meters on Kurzebracker Weg, turn right onto the woodland path that heads south along the Erlengraben forest creek. Follow this path for 600 meters to the Erlengrabeenteich, a small and secluded forest pond. Take the path to the right back onto Hennigsdorfer Straße and head south on Hennigsdorger Straße for 450 meters.

At Alt-Heiligensee, turn right and head into the old village center. This well-preserved and secluded suburb, with its cobbled roads, 15th-century village church, ironmonger, and string of vintage shops will call to mind long-ago village life.

Keep following the Alt-Heiligensee road clockwise past the village center as it divides the Havel River from the Heiligensee. You can access the beach at the Seebad Heiligensee Gaststätte, where even just the view across the water is worth the trip. After the Sandhauserbrücke, carry on for 900 meters on Sandhauser Straße before turning left on Rallenweg and heading into Tegeler Forst.

Descend into the green oasis beneath the rich canopy above, following the forest road for 300 meters. Take the second left, and after 200 meters you'll approach the Baumberge, a sandy dune landscape that

Höchster Baum Berlins

Buche

Höhe: 43,15 m

Durchmesser: 0,96 m

1843 gepflanzt

Stand: 7.7.2022

occupies the wood's middle ground. Head east across the dunes for 500 meters; then, at the first forest junction, turn right and head south back to the main forest road. Turn left and head east; after 500 meters, you'll come upon the city's tallest tree. No need to worry—the tree is heavily signposted, so there is no chance of missing it.

After 1.5 kilometers, the forest path crosses the Schwarzer Weg before arriving at Dicke Marie—named by Wilhelm and Alexander von Humboldt, who grew up nearby—opposite the placid waters of the Tegelersee. Follow the leafy lakeside path for a kilometer as it curves around the Archaic Archangel of Heiligensee statue on the peninsula. From here, you can see all the way to Spandau across the stunningly clear water. Just across the lake is the Borsig Villa.

Follow the path east for 300 meters and then head south across the impressive maroon-red steel Tegeler Hafenbrücke (Tegel Harbor Bridge) and onto the lakeside Greenwich Promenade. You'll see locals sauntering along this relaxing walkway, drinking beers, and admiring the ducks as boats set off to cruise around the city's waterways.

Follow the Greenwich Promenade to the south, past the 18th-century cannons, through the woods, and across the Borsigdammbrücke. One kilometer after leaving the Greenwich Promenade, turn left on Neheimer Straße, passing huge murals on the building facades. After 200 meters on Neheimer Straße, turn right on Namslaustraße and continue for one kilometer. Then, turn left on Berliner Straße and follow it into the heart of Tegel. After 900 meters, turn left on Am Borsigturm and follow it westward into the area's former steelworking district. After 500 meters, turn right and head north onto Medebacher Weg. You'll find Kubi's Point on the right just before Brunowplatz.

KUBI'S POINT

The lush and sprawling residential district of Tegel was sadly lacking a craft-beer bar before the arrival of Kubi's Point in 2017. Homey, with an excellent and welcoming staff, the bar is decorated with beer memorabilia from around the world. The team here champions Berlin's brewing community, and from the fridge you can select beers from any number of local manufacturers (which are, of course, covered in this book). Kubi's Point started its own brewing in 2022 to positive acclaim—just ask the countless locals who drink here. The bar's seven taps always include Messing (the Kubi's Point Pilsner), a rotating seasonal beer, and other local brews. Highlights of the year at Kubi's include kitchen takeovers, beer tasting sessions, and film screenings.

ADDRESS

Kubi's Point
Medebacher Weg 14
Alt-Tegel
13507 Berlin
+49 177 3163999
kubanek@kubis-point.de
www.kubis-point.de

Photos © Yvonne Hartmann

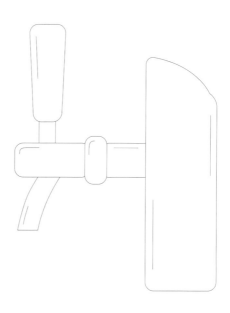

WEST BERLIN

FROM GRUNEWALD TO SIEMENSSTADT

GRUNEWALD, BERLIN

▷··· STARTING POINT	···✕ DESTINATION
GRUNEWALD S-BAHN STATION	**FUERST WIACEK**
🍺 BEER NAME	🏛 DIFFICULTY
AFTER PARTY	**MODERATE**
🚃 TRANSPORT	🕐 DURATION
S3, S5, S7	**2.5 H**
⛰ ZONE	↦ LENGTH
B	**11.5 KM**
🔍 HIGHLIGHTS	⤳ ELEVATION GAIN
DRACHENBERG, OLYMPIASTADION, SIEMENS TOWER	ASCENT: 110 M DESCENT: 130 M

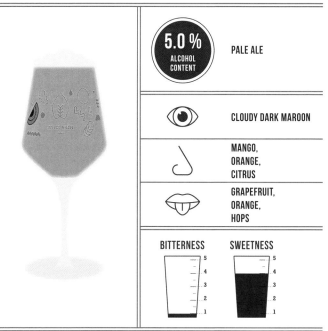

5.0 %
ALCOHOL CONTENT

PALE ALE

CLOUDY DARK MAROON

MANGO,
ORANGE,
CITRUS

GRAPEFRUIT,
ORANGE,
HOPS

BITTERNESS

SWEETNESS

AFTER PARTY. A captivating pale ale that's rich in fruity aromas and flavors, yet still light enough to not overwhelm the senses.

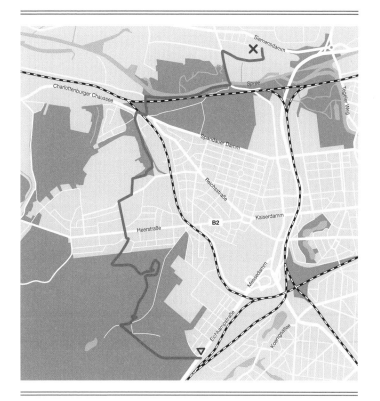

HIKE DESCRIPTION

Stretching out along the river Havel in the city's western district, Grunewald is the biggest forest in Berlin. Amidst its 3,000 hectares, you'll find an interconnected series of freshwater lakes, multiple hills for looking out across the city, lots of hidden restaurants, and even an old Cold War spy tower. This scenic woodland area is prime hiking territory for Berliners and provides the perfect starting point for our walk.

Head west out of the station, taking the first footpath on the left into the forest (Schildhornweg). Stay on the path and walk straight for one kilometer and then head northwest along the garden allotments until you reach Teufelsseechaussee. Turn right on Teufelsseechaussee and either follow it for 1.3 kilometers to the Drachenberg carpark or deviate onto one of the footpaths in the woodlands on the other side of the road, heading upward and in a northeasterly direction until you arrive at the same destination.

Either take the stairs or ascend the path that climbs up and around to the top of Drachenberg, a huge mound made from rubble collected after the Second World War. From here you can see across the whole city and over to Teufelsberg, where the domes of a Cold War listening station can be seen on the horizon.

Descend the opposite side of Drachenberg and take the first right, which will lead you further down through the woodlands and past the bottom of a winter toboggan run, after which the path bends to the left; follow it for another 200 meters, turn right into the woods, and take the first right once again to emerge at Tapiauer Allee.

Leaving the forest on Tapiauer Allee, turn left on Lyckallee and then right on Kranzallee. Cross Heerstraße and walk up Flatowallee toward the Olympiastadion. Turn right just after the Olympiastadion S-Bahn station and follow Trakehner Allee until you hit Gutsmuthsweg; turn left and follow Gutsmuthsweg to the stadium's monumental facade. This colossal and impressive structure, built for the 1936 Summer Olympics, is worth a visit any time of the year.

Head east, away from the stadium on Olympischer Platz, and turn left on Rossitter Weg, heading toward the Olympia-Stadion U-Bahn station. Turn left on Rominter Allee and follow it for 1.4 kilometers. Then turn right on Spandauer Damm and take the first left onto Wiesendamm. After 250 meters, take the first right after crossing the rail tracks and follow the path that runs between the green allotments and the Spree River.

Follow the wooded riverside path for 1.5 kilometers and then cross the Rohrdammbrücke. Head north on Rohrdamm for 500 meters, entering the industrial area of Siemenstadt. Turn right on Wohlrabedamm, passing the former Siemens industrial complex and residential tower as you head deeper into the industrial area. After 750 meters, follow the road to the left, pass beneath the disused U-Bahn railway, and arrive at the former Wernerwerk station, opposite which you'll find the entrance to the Fuerst Wiacek brewery.

FUERST WIACEK

Fuerst Wiacek is unquestionably one of the most exciting and highly regarded breweries in the whole of Germany. The relatively new operation was founded in 2016 by Georg Fürst and Lukasz Wiacek, who started making a name for themselves with their full-flavored hazy IPAs before branching out into a large variety of different beers, including Pilsners, sours, porters, and more, with new beers introduced to the assortment on a weekly basis. In just a few years they've amassed a fan base throughout Europe thanks to their meticulously brewed beers and creative branding. The brewery, alas, doesn't have a taproom, but there are regular openings, events, and tours on offer, so check the website for more information. Fuerst Wiacek beers are served up in many of Berlin's taprooms, and on-site pickups are possible on Friday afternoons.

ADDRESS

Fuerst Wiacek GmbH
Wohlrabedamm 3
13629 Berlin
+49 152 23779829
hey@fuerstwiacek.com
www.fuerstwiacek.com

Photos © Yvonne Hartmann

SOUTH BERLIN

DOGWALK

A JOURNEY THROUGH BERLIN'S INDUSTRIAL PAST

MARIENDORF, BERLIN

▷⋯ STARTING POINT	⋯✕ DESTINATION
SÜDKREUZ S-BAHN STATION	**BREWDOG DOGTAP**
🍶 BEER NAME	🀫 DIFFICULTY
ELVIS JUICE	**MODERATE**
🚆 TRANSPORT	🕓 DURATION
RINGBAHN	**2 H**
⛰ ZONE	↦ LENGTH
A	**9 KM**
🔎 HIGHLIGHTS	〰 ELEVATION GAIN
TELTOW CANAL, MARIENDORFER HAFENSTEG	ASCENT: 15 M DESCENT: 10 M

5.1 % ALCOHOL CONTENT	IPA
👁	AMBER
👃	GRAPEFRUIT, ORANGE PINE
👄	GRAPEFRUIT, CARAMEL

BITTERNESS	SWEETNESS
5 4 3 2 1	5 4 3 2 1

ELVIS JUICE. A classically brewed IPA with strong grapefruit and orange flavors, a mild bitterness, and a sweet caramel character.

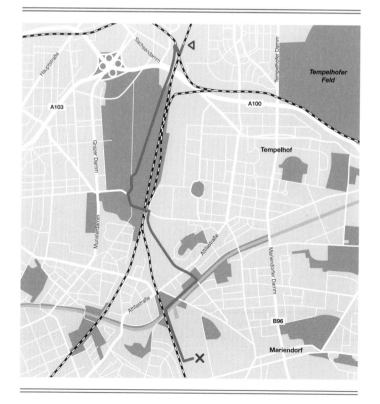

HIKE DESCRIPTION

Trust us, you've never been to a BrewDog like this one. The brewery and the headquarters of Brew-Dog's European business activities are all contained within a giant, red brick gasworks that dates back to 1901. This hike takes you through a unique Berlin neighborhood filled with relics of the city's industrial past. You'll cross disused industrial railway lines and walk beside the old Teltow Canal.

Leaving the station through the main entrance, take an immediate left and follow the unnamed walkway and bicycle path that leads you south over the highway into the gardens and greens of Hans-Baluschek Park.

The expansive grassy area is bordered by private allotments to the west and a nature reserve to the east. Reach this award-winning park and former railyard, known as Schöneberger Südgelände, by crossing the old steel bridge over the still-functioning tracks. This one-of-a-kind reserve is filled with vintage train memorabilia from the old Berlin–Dresden line, artworks, and ecological areas—a blend of history, green space, and contemporary culture.

After walking for 2 kilometers, you'll reach the edge of the park at Priesterweg. Proceed down Priesterweg until you hit Prellerweg. Turn left on Prellerweg, cross under a disused iron bridge, and continue until you reach Röblingstraße. Take a right and follow Röblingstraße south for a kilometer, walking parallel to more disused railway tracks.

After crossing Attilastraße, Röblingstraße turns into Gersdorfstraße, which brings you to the Teltow Canal. Take the path on the northern embankment of the canal. Follow the canal southwest for a kilometer and reach Mariendorfer-Hafen-Steg, a picturesque public footbridge made from cast steel girders and wooden planks.

Across the bridge, a small public footpath will take you further south along the train tracks. As you approach the Mariendorf Industrial Park, you'll see the old gasholder looming in the distance, signaling your approach to the BrewDog brewery and garden.

BREWDOG DOGTAP

BrewDog's European headquarters is easily one of the best craft-beer bars in Berlin. The 2,500-square-meter space has 25 taps serving up a vast variety of beers. The space is epic, with stained-glass windows suggesting you've just entered a giant, secret beer-church. There's also a bowling alley, a minigolf course, arcade machines, a beer museum, a gift shop, and the opportunity to take a tour of the brewery. The outdoor space is just as impressive, with a huge garden, seating area and an outdoor bar. The food is modern and quite anglicized, with burgers and wings making up much of the menu, all done up in charac- teristic BrewDog style with plenty of vegetarian and vegan options.

ADDRESS

BrewDog DogTap
Im Marienpark 23
12107 Berlin
+49 30 21234347
dogtapberlin@brewdog.com
www.brewdog.com/uk/dogtap-berlin

Photos © Yvonne Hartmann

LANDWEHR CANAL

A BOHEMIAN WATERSIDE STROLL

KREUZBERG,
BERLIN

▷··· STARTING POINT	···✕ DESTINATION
HALLESCHES TOR U-BAHN STATION	**SCHOPPE BRÄU TAPROOM IM BKK**
🍺 BEER NAME	❖ DIFFICULTY
SOMMERMÄRCHEN	**EASY**
🚈 TRANSPORT	🕐 DURATION
U1, U3, U6	**1 H**
⛰ ZONE	↦ LENGTH
A	**4.9 KM**
🔍 HIGHLIGHTS	〰 ELEVATION GAIN
LANDWEHRKANAL, ADMIRALBRÜCKE, KOTTBUSSER BRÜCKE	ASCENT: 10 M DESCENT: 10 M

WEISSBIER

ORANGE

**PINEAPPLE,
HERB**

**SWEET FRUITS,
CARAMEL,
HOPS**

BITTERNESS   SWEETNESS

SOMMERMÄRCHEN. From the first go, the fruity aromas and flavors of this light and summery wheat beer wow the palate.

HIKE DESCRIPTION

One of the highlights of Berlin's Kreuzberg district is the old industrial canal that cuts through the heart of the city from Tiergarten to Friedrichshain. During the summer months, the waterway morphs into a playground for city residents, full of inflatable boats, tourist ships, and floating restaurants. Walking along the canal you'll see Turkish markets, a plethora of bars and restaurants, and some of the city's most welcoming and bohemian neighborhoods, where you can find everything from vegan doughnuts to take-away kofta dishes and more.

Exiting Hallesches Tor onto Hallesche-Tor-Brücke, head east on Waterloo-Ufer on the south side of the canal. Pass Zossener Brücke and follow the footpath that runs along the water's edge, passing the old and colorful pumping station on the other side of the canal.

Cross Waterloobrücke and take the canalside footpath to your right. Walk around the old tollhouse, cross Prinzenstraße, and follow the path to Admiralbrücke. The path will take you past moored boats, restaurants, and bevies of swans patrolling the grassy embankment. Admiralbrücke has become a haven for the city's beatniks, who gather here most evenings to play music, drink beer, and watch the sunset across the water.

Continue on Planufer to Kottbusser Brücke. Cross over Kottbusser Brücke and walk along Maybachufer, which on Tuesdays and Fridays turns into a grand bazaar featuring farmers' food stalls, a wide variety of international cuisines, and textile vendors. Follow Maybachufer eastward until you reach the junction with Pannierstraße (about a kilometer). Cross Thielenbrücke to the other side of the canal and take an immediate left at the pavilion, following the canalside path. Heading west along Paul-Lincke-Ufer, you'll see locals sitting by the water, boutique cafés, and even a boules court.

As the path runs further west, the setting becomes more village-like, with cobbled roads and classical architecture. About a kilometer after passing Thielenbrücke, turn right onto Manteuffelstraße and follow it for 250 meters, crossing Reichenbergerstraße, to reach the BKK taproom—aka Bier Kombinat Kreuzberg—on your left.

SCHOPPE BRÄU TAPROOM IM BKK

If there's one thing the Schoppe team aren't afraid of, it's flavor. Head brewer Thorsten Schoppe is regarded as one of the instigators of the reinvigorated craft-beer movement in Berlin, and working your way through his beer menu, you'll see why. On offer are full-bodied IPAs, Witbiers, Dunkels, Lagers, Bocks, Pilsners, and more, each one rich in character and taste. The brewery is in the city center, but Schoppe decided to set up a taproom in the Kreuzberg district, just off the Landwehr Canal. The bar itself is very no-nonsense. Tasting sessions are offered weekly, brewery visits are possible, and brewing courses are bookable through the Schoppe website.

ADDRESS

Schoppe Bräu Taproom im BKK
Manteuffelstraße 53
10999 Berlin
+49 175 2468103
www.schoppebraeu.de

Photos © Yvonne Hartmann

KREUZBERG TOUR

A HISTORICAL STROLL THROUGH BERLIN'S MOST FAMOUS DISTRICT

KREUZBERG, BERLIN

▷··· STARTING POINT	···✕ DESTINATION
PLATZ DER LUFTBRÜCKE U-BAHN STATION	**BRAUHAUS SÜDSTERN**
🍺 BEER NAME	🁢 DIFFICULTY
ORANG UTAN ALE	**EASY**
🚃 TRANSPORT	🕐 DURATION
U6	**1 H**
⛰ ZONE	↦ LENGTH
A	**5 KM**
🔍 HIGHLIGHTS	〰 ELEVATION GAIN
PLATZ DER LUFTBRÜCKE, VIKTORIA PARK, BERGMANNSTRASSE, MARHEINEKE MARKET HALL, BERGMANNSTRASSE CHURCH	ASCENT: 30 M DESCENT: 40 M

PALE ALE

COPPER WITH WHITE
CREAMY HEAD

MALTY,
HOPS,
DRIED FRUIT

HERBY,
DRIED FRUIT

BITTERNESS SWEETNESS

ORANG UTAN ALE. A caramelized rustic red ale rich in tropical flavors
that is brewed especially to raise money for the Borneo Orangutan
Survival charity.

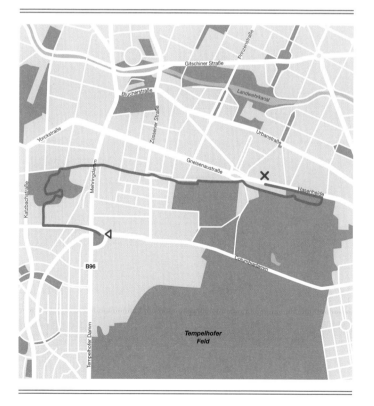

HIKE DESCRIPTION

Located in the center of the city, Kreuzberg is one of Berlin's best-known districts. Starting at the historic Platz der Luftbrücke, this walk ventures off to the 66-meter-high hill at Viktoria Park—the "Berg" from which the district gets its name—via the lively Bergmannstraße.

The memorial at the Platz der Luftbrücke honors the pilots who died while bringing in supplies for the Berlin population during the Soviet blockade in 1948. From here, you'll walk west down Dudenstraße to the south entrance of Viktoria Park, passing the old Schultheiß brewery, which has now been converted into a residential area. A tree-lined path leads you up the steps into Viktoria Park. Beyond the sports fields on

your right, you can see across into the whole of Kreuzberg. Keep right at the end of the steps and follow the path up to the summit, straight toward the National Monument.

The history of this 12.8-hectare park began in 1821 with the inauguration of the Prussian Monument for the Liberation Wars, designed by Karl Friedrich Schinke and dedicated to German victories in the Wars of Liberation against Napoleon. It's worth going up the steps to this Neo-Gothic monument to take in the view across the city.

On the way down, keep to the left and then take the second turn to the right, which will lead you past a large lawn and shady trees to the pond. From the pond, take the first turn left, which will take you down a few steps and over a small bridge to the animal park. Continue along the path to the right, following the stream to the park exit.

Here, next to the bronze sculpture at the foot of a waterfall (a replica of the Hainfall in Poland), you'll have a wonderful view up through the treetops to the monument at the top of the park.

Leave the park on its northern side and continue east on Kreuzberg-straße until you reach Mehringdamm. For a little refreshment or even a good meal, we recommend a beer-stop at the Dolden Mädel Braugast-haus before you cross Mehringdamm and head straight into bustling Bergmannstraße.

With its many boutiques, cafés, restaurants, and galleries, the colorful Bergmannstraße is truly the heart of the neighborhood. Follow the street and let yourself drift. After 600 meters, you'll see the Marheineke Markthalle on your left, with its rich variety of international culinary delicacies.

Walk 200 meters further down Bergmannstraße, passing the Passion Church, to the entrance of the cemetery complex. Enter the cemetery, and for the next 500 meters enjoy the tranquility of the idyllic church-yard as you walk eastward parallel to Bergmannstraße. When you reach Café Strauß, return to Bergmannstraße, which you'll follow for a few hundred meters to the east again, until you reach the church at Südstern. Follow Hasenheide east for 300 meters and you'll arrive at the outdoor terrace of Brauhaus Südstern.

BRAUHAUS SÜDSTERN

At Brauhaus Südstern, the brewmaster uses a traditional gentle process to brew fresh, unfiltered, and natural beers that retain their full character and taste. In addition to the classic light and dark styles, the tangy Stern Weiße and the spicy-fruity Orang Utan Ale are served up all year round, with specialties such as Märzen, Festbier, and Bockbier available depending on the season. With a grand terrace, beer garden, spacious interior, and stage, the brewery has plenty of space for music and private events. It also offers regular tours and brewing courses.

ADDRESS

Brauhaus Südstern
Hasenheide 69
10967 Berlin
+49 30 69001624
info@brauhaus-suedstern.de
www.brauhaus-suedstern.de

Photos © Yvonne Hartmann

TEMPELHOF TOUR

WALKING ACROSS THE WORLD'S MOST FAMOUS AIRSTRIP

NEUKÖLLN-KREUZ-
BERG, BERLIN

▷··· STARTING POINT	···✕ DESTINATION
SÜDSTERN U-BAHN STATION	BRAUHAUS NEULICH
BEER NAME	DIFFICULTY
NEULICH ORIGINAL	EASY
TRANSPORT	DURATION
U7	40 MIN.
ZONE	LENGTH
A	3.2 KM
HIGHLIGHTS	ELEVATION GAIN
VOLKSPARK HASENHEIDE TEMPELHOF AIRPORT, SCHILLERKEUZ	ASCENT: 20 M DESCENT: 10 M

4.9 % ALCOHOL CONTENT	ALE
	LIGHT AMBER
	MALT, SWEET FRUITS
	HOPS, BITTER, CITRUS

BITTERNESS	SWEETNESS
5 4 3 2 1	5 4 3 2 1

 NEULICH ORIGINAL. A light summer ale with a mild fruity flavor profile.

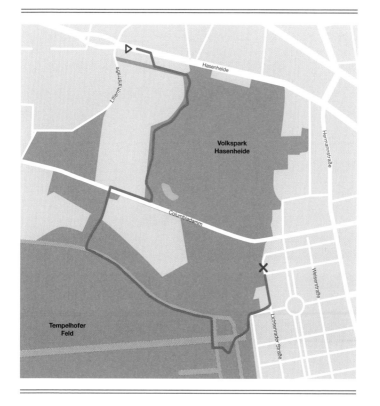

HIKE DESCRIPTION

It's not often you get to walk down the runway of a world-famous airport. Because Berlin ended up with too many airports, however, Tempelhof was forced to shut back in 2008, and the airstrip and accompanying land were given back to the public. Where Allied forces once flew in supplies for West Berlin during the famous Airlift, you'll now find a field dotted with public gardens, nature preserves, and spaces for kite flying, skating, and film screenings. Meanwhile, simply walking across the runway is like taking a step through history.

From the station, head east on Hasenheide. Take a short detour through Brauhaus Südstern and into Hasenheide park. Walking in an easterly direction, take a right at the memorial for the Trümmerfrauen—the women whose role it was to clear up the rubble after the Second World War.

Heading deeper into Hasenheide and past the dog park, take a right at the first junction and follow the little wooded path until you reach Columbiadamm. Take a right on Columbiadamm, head west for 250 meters, and reach the entrance to Tempelhofer Feld. As you enter the repurposed park, you'll see the old airport to your right (along with a grazing area for sheep).

Follow the curving taxiway clockwise, navigating your way past the cyclists, roller skaters, and runners. After a kilometer, the taxiway meets the 2-kilometer-long runway. This very intersection has been converted into an urban gardening area where residents can grow their own flowers and vegetables.

From the end of the runway, continue east to the edge of the park and then head north for 150 meters to the Herrfurthstraße-Oderstraße entrance. Leave the park and follow Herrfurthstraße to the right into the bohemian Schillerkiez district of Berlin. After a few hundred meters, turn left on Lichtenraderstraße; you'll soon see Brauhaus Neulich's outdoor guests. You have arrived at one of Neukölln's finest craft-beer bars.

BRAUHAUS NEULICH

This new addition to the Berlin brewing scene fits right into its young and trendy neighborhood. The Neulich team's bright, creative energy can be felt in the beer's vibey spirit and the exciting atmosphere that characterizes the bar. It's a space rich in ambience, powered sustainably by the brewery's own wind turbine!

To complement the Original and Helles that are on offer all year round, the team regularly changes out their tap menu with new seasonal concoctions and collaborations. Just like the Original, the Bock beer packs a punch!

With its regular musical events and a menu supplied by the dumpling restaurant next door, Brauhaus Neulich has become one of the most exciting and fresh faces of Berlin's beer scene.

ADDRESS

Brauhaus Neulich GmbH
Selchower Straße 20
12049 Berlin
+49 33 17043211
info@brauhaus-neulich.de
www.brauhaus-neulich.de

Photos © Yvonne Hartmann

BRANDENBURG

ALTLANDSBERG

HIKE TO AN ANCIENT PRUSSIAN PALACE

ALTLANDSBERG, BRANDENBURG

▷··· STARTING POINT	···✗ DESTINATION
NEUENHAGEN S-BAHN STATION	**SBB ALTLANDSBERG**
🍺 BEER NAME	🎲 DIFFICULTY
ALTLANDSBERGER KUPFER	**MODERATE**
🚆 TRANSPORT	🕐 DURATION
S5	**2 H**
⛰ ZONE	↦ LENGTH
C	**8.5 KM**
🔍 HIGHLIGHTS	〰 ELEVATION GAIN
SCHLOSSGUT ALTLANDSBERG, BERLINER TORTURM, STADTPFARRKIRCHE ST. MARIEN	ASCENT: 50 M DESCENT: 30 M

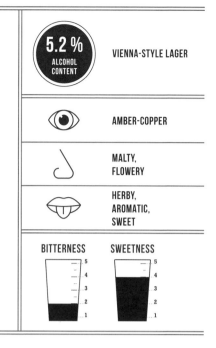

5.2 %
ALCOHOL
CONTENT

VIENNA-STYLE LAGER

AMBER-COPPER

MALTY,
FLOWERY

HERBY,
AROMATIC,
SWEET

BITTERNESS

SWEETNESS

 ALTLANDSBERGER KUPFER. A sweet and mildly aromatic lager, bold in character and featuring subtle flavors of nut and toffee.

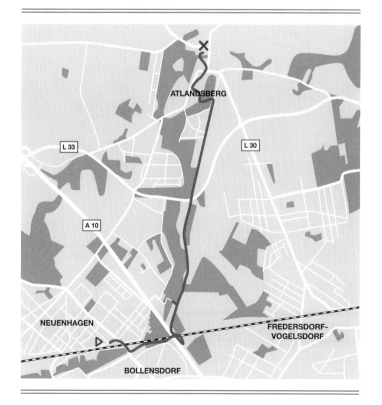

ATLANDSBERG

L 33

L 30

A 10

NEUENHAGEN

FREDERSDORF-
VOGELSDORF

BOLLENSDORF

HIKE DESCRIPTION

The historic Prussian manor house located in the rustic village of Altlandsberg is one of the region's most pristine and beautiful landmarks. Originally built by Baron Otto von Schwerin, the estate was eventually passed down to the Prussian King Friedrich I, who used it as one of his many residences. The elegant, recently renovated manor house offers an escape from the city on a walk that takes you through a serene landscape of gently rolling fields.

Coming out of the station, follow Eisenbahnstraße to the east, cross Hauptstraße, and go northeast on Fichtestraße until you pass beneath a highway bridge. Follow the road you are on, now called Am Wall, as it bends to the right. At the first junction, continue straight ahead on Elisenhof (Am Wall turns left). After crossing the Erpe, continue to follow Elisenhof as it makes a ninety-degree turn to the left at the next T-junction. You'll now be heading north roughly parallel to the Erpe.

As you continue northward, you'll pass horse sanctuaries, stables, and farmyards. The country road, now called Wiesengrund, passes beneath another highway as you make your way through the fields.

As you enter the town of Altlandsberg, countryside cottages and sports fields start to appear. If doing the hike during the off-season, you'll see fields full of water buffalo who pasture here during the winter.

On Bollendorfersweg (the continuation of Wiesengrund), as you pass a giant field to your left, there'll be a signposted country path directing you to the town center. Follow this path, cross a little brook, and carry on as the path takes you between the cemetery and town hall.

Take a right on Berliner Allee, while taking note of the historic imperial post office on your left. After a few hundred meters, you'll arrive at the Berliner Torturm, a 14th-century tower that formed part of the town's historic defensive wall.

Carry on into the medieval town along the cobblestone streets until you reach Hirtengasse. Follow Hirtengasse until you get to Klosterstraße, where you'll take a left into the old village square.

Carry on for a few hundred meters on Klosterstraße, cross over Strausberger Straße, and continue on Bernauer Straße. You'll arrive at the medieval church of St. Marien, which was built in the 13th century.

Walk counterclockwise around the church and reach Berliner Straße. Turn right and head directly past the Schlosskirche and into the grounds of Schlossgut Altlandsberg, where you'll see signs discussing the history and previous residents of the manor. If you're lucky, you might even catch a glimpse of the Nachtwächter (night watchman) guiding people around the estate. You'll find the brewery and restaurant in a red brick building overlooking the pleasure gardens.

SBB ALTLANDSBERG

Originally built by Schloss Altlandsberg's Baron Otto von Schwerin, this brewery is easily one of the oldest in the region, dating back to 1659. After the palace's restoration in 2016, the brewery became an integral part of the palace grounds. A Helles, a Kupfer, and a Dunkel are on tap throughout the year; all of them are quite herby, with varying levels of sweetness. The brewery also specializes in seasonal beers, with a particularly noteworthy Maibock. The restaurant serves home-cooked traditional German dishes and cakes and features views across the palace gardens. There's also a distillery on-site that produces great liquors, gins, and schnapps using ecologically produced local ingredients.

ADDRESS

Sozietätsbrauerei und Brennerei Altlandsberg AG
Krummenseestraße 2
15345 Altlandsberg
+49 33 17043211
www.schlossgut-altlandsberg.de

Photos © Yvonne Hartmann

SANSSOUCI

A STROLL THROUGH HISTORICAL PRUSSIAN GARDENS

POTSDAM,
BRANDENBURG

▷⋯ STARTING POINT	⋯✕ DESTINATION
BAHNHOF POTSDAM PARK SANSSOUCI	**MEIEREI IM NEUEN GARTEN**
🍺 BEER NAME	🁢 DIFFICULTY
MEIEREI ROTBIER	**EASY**
🚋 TRANSPORT	🕐 DURATION
RE 1	**2.5 H**
⛰ ZONE	↦ LENGTH
C	**7.8 KM**
🔎 HIGHLIGHTS	〰 ELEVATION GAIN
SCHLOSS SANSSOUCI, NEUES PALAIS	ASCENT: 30 M DESCENT: 30 M

ROTBIER

COPPER WITH WHITE
CREAMY HEAD

MALTY,
HOPS,
DRIED FRUIT

HERBY,
DRIED FRUIT

BITTERNESS

SWEETNESS

 MEIEREI ROTBIER. A rich and full-bodied red malt ale with dried fruit flavors that continue to develop on the palate long after the initial tasting.

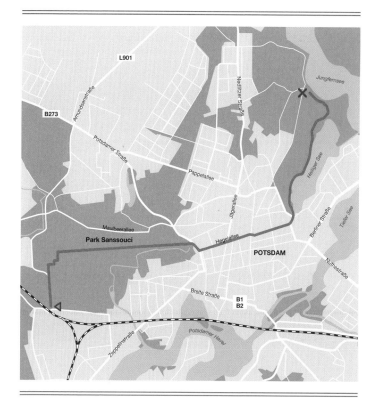

HIKE DESCRIPTION

The UNESCO-protected baroque gardens and palaces of Sanssouci, situated just outside of Berlin in the city of Potsdam, were once used by Prussian royalty as a private retreat. This gentle stroll takes you past the centuries-old regal dwellings, through the regional capital, and to the immaculately preserved Neuer Garten. Here, among many other majestic properties, you'll find the Cecilienhof Palace, which played host to the Potsdam Conference in 1945.

Coming out of Bahnhof Potsdam Park Sanssouci, head north on Am Neuen Palais until you enter the palatial grounds; follow the path until you reach the Neues Palais.

To the right, the main park pathway, Hauptallee, takes you from here past the banquet halls straight to the iconic Sanssouci Palace, which sits above the gardens' terraced vineyards. After 2 kilometers, head straight on out of the park, turn right on Schopenhauerstraße and follow it for a few hundred meters; then take a left on Hegelallee and proceed straight through Potsdam's historic city center for 1.5 kilometers to Neuer Garten (after Nauener Tor, Hegelallee becomes Kurfürstenstraße).

The Neuer Garten, Potsdam's second park, was established by Friedrich Wilhelm II, who wanted to create a more modern space than Sanssouci. Upon entering the park, take the lakeside path past the Gothic Library to the pristine Marble Palace (about a kilometer).

The path continues past the Heiliger See and ends at the Grünes Haus, which looks out across the lake. With the Cecilienhof Palace to your left, circumnavigate the Grünes Haus and head northward for a few hundred meters to the shores of the Jungfernsee. The path then heads

in a westerly direction, hugging the lake's shore. The path continues for just under a kilometer before arriving at the entrance to the former dairy, today the Meierei brewhouse.

MEIEREI IM NEUEN GARTEN

This majestic lakeside brewery was originally built as a dairy to serve royal residents in the 18th century—hence its name, the "Dairy in the New Garden." The first restaurant to use this space closed in 1945; the building was then restored after German reunification, and the brewery and current restaurant opened in 2003. Today the Brauerei seats over 200 people, and its beer garden offers stunning views across the water. Inside, the restaurant is decked out like a traditional Prussian tavern, with a menu befitting the period in which it was originally built. The on-site brewery takes its seasonal specialties very seriously, changing up its award-winning menu regularly; Weizen and Bock beers are always on offer, as is the trademark Rotbier.

ADDRESS

Gasthausbrauerei Meierei im Neuen Garten GmbH
Im Neuen Garten 10
14469 Potsdam
+49 33 17043211
www.meierei-potsdam.de

Photos © Daniel Cole

THEODOR-FONTANE-WEG

LAKES, BEACHES & BRANDENBURG VILLAGES

WOLTERSDORF, BRANDENBURG

▷┄ STARTING POINT	┄✕ DESTINATION
ERKNER S-BAHN STATION	WOLTERSDORFER SCHLEUSENBRAUEREI
🍺 BEER NAME	🍺 DIFFICULTY
WOLTERSDORFER DUNKEL	**MODERATE**
🚋 TRANSPORT	🕐 DURATION
S3	**2 H**
⛰ ZONE	↦ LENGTH
C	**10 KM**
🔎 HIGHLIGHTS	〜 ELEVATION GAIN
THEODOR-FONTANE-WEG, WOLTERSDORFER SCHLEUSE, BADESTELLE WOLTERSDORFER KALKSEE	ASCENT: 50 M DESCENT: 50 M

5.0 % ALCOHOL CONTENT	DUNKLES
👁	DARK BROWN
👃	COFFEE, DARK MALTS
👅	COFFEE, CHOCOLATE

BITTERNESS

5
4
3
2
1

SWEETNESS

5
4
3
2
1

WOLTERSDORFER DUNKEL. A light yet full-bodied dark beer with notes of coffee and roasted malt that doesn't overwhelm your palate.

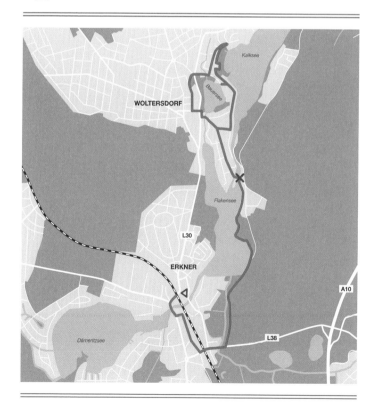

HIKE DESCRIPTION

Pack your swimwear and get ready to visit some of the area's nicest lakes and beaches! The Theodor-Fontane-Weg—part of a series of walkways dedicated to the famous German writer—runs along three stunning bodies of water (the Bauersee, Flakensee, and Kalksee) with several beaches offering perfect spots to swim. Starting in Erkner on the Berlin border, the hike passes through woodlands, camping sites, and quaint villages with cobbled streets. It's hard to believe that you're just a 20-minute train ride from Berlin's city center.

As you leave the station, turn right onto Bahnhofstraße. At the traffic circle, take a left on Friedrichstraße, and cross the Flakenfließ River. Take the first left on Beuststraße and then the first right onto Ernst-Thälmann-Straße and walk south until you reach Fürstenwalder Straße. Take a left and follow Fürstenwalder Straße until you reach the sign-posted Theodor-Fontane-Weg on your left (about 450 meters). Follow the Theodor-Fontane-Weg to the north into the woods.

On wooden stands beside the forested path you'll find poems by local authors inspired by the various trees around you. (The trail is also known as the Poetry Path.) After walking along the water for 20 minutes you'll arrive at the first beach, a natural sandy spot full of locals and ice cream vendors. Not long afterward, the path arrives at a promenade leading into the serene, Tuscan-like village of Woltersdorf.

Cross the lock separating the Flakensee from the Kalksee; then follow Schleusenstraße north as it runs parallel to a quaint tram line, which dates back to 1915. After 800 meters, turn right on Parkstraße; then turn left on Kalkseestraße and head north for 1.5 kilometers (Kalkseestraße has in the meantime become Schubertstraße and then Richard-Wagner-Straße) until you reach the next swimming opportunity: the Woltersdorf Kalksee beach.

Retrace your steps on Richard-Wagner-Straße for 130 meters, turn right on Beethovenstraße and right again on Interlakenstraße, and then turn left on Rüdersdorfer Straße. As you head south, stop to make the most of the magnificent and serene views across the Bauersee. Take a left on Rudolf-Breitscheid-Straße and follow the tramline back toward the locks, where you'll find the Woltersdorfer Braugasthaus on the water's edge.

WOLTERSDORFER SCHLEUSENBRAUEREI

You'll struggle to find a brewery located in a more beautiful setting. Looking out across the Flakensee and surrounded by woodlands in a quaint countryside village, the Schleusenbrauerei is as charming and peaceful as they come. With an extensive beer garden perched on the edge of the lake and a classic German pub menu befitting the setting (Knödel, herring sandwich, and currywurst), this traditional bar and restaurant is the perfect destination for lazy summer day excursions. With several different beers on tap—a Helles, a Dunkel, a Weizen, and a rotating special—there's always something on offer for a beer hiker here.

ADDRESS

Woltersdorfer Braugasthaus
An der Schleuse 2b
15569 Woltersdorf
+49 33 628862296
www.woltersdorfer.com

Photos © Daniel Cole

EINSTEIN ROAD

A WOODLAND ESCAPADE THROUGH POTSDAM'S RURAL BACKCOUNTRY

TEMPLIN, BRANDENBURG

▷··· STARTING POINT	···✕ DESTINATION
POTSDAM HAUPTBAHNHOF	**FORSTHAUS TEMPLIN**
🍺 BEER NAME	🔢 DIFFICULTY
POTSDAMER STANGE	**MODERATE**
🚆 TRANSPORT	⏲ DURATION
RE1, S7	**3 H 45 MIN.**
⛰ ZONE	↦ LENGTH
C	**13.5 KM**
🔍 HIGHLIGHTS	〰 ELEVATION GAIN
EINSTEIN TOWER, KLEINER RAVENSBERG, EINSTEIN'S SUMMER HOUSE	ASCENT: 180 M DESCENT: 160 M

4.5 % ALCOHOL CONTENT	POTSDAMER STANGE

 DARK CLOUDY YELLOW

 LIGHT CITRUS, MALTS, FLOWERY

 BANANA, HERBS, FLORAL, BITTER

BITTERNESS

SWEETNESS

 POTSDAMER STANGE. This unfiltered organic beer, which is unique to this region, is made using exclusively local ingredients. Rich in flavor and served in a custom glass, this mildly bitter, fruity brew tastes like something between a wheat beer and a smooth, light pilsner.

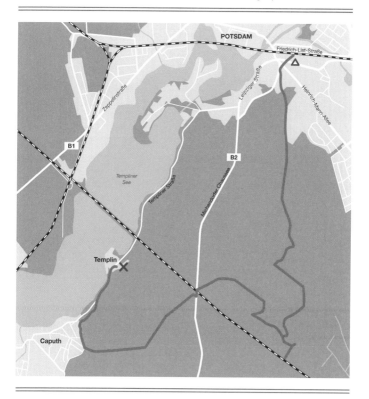

HIKE DESCRIPTION

A small summer house once inhabited by Albert Einstein is nestled away alongside the Templinersee in the village of Caputh. The famous physicist, who once lived and studied in Berlin, left behind an important legacy in this part of Germany. A science park, a tower, and an observatory named after him are located just south of the Potsdam city center.

Leaving the station, head south for 500 meters on the Brauhausberg road—Potsdam's old brewery hill. Just before the bridge that arches over the road, a set of stairs will take you up onto the hillside. Once at the top, cross the bridge over Brauhausberg and arrive at the aptly named Albert-Einstein-Straße. Follow this road south into the woods, passing the Albert Einstein science park while keeping an eye out for the observatory that also bears the famous physicist's name.

As you enter the woods, take note of the painted white squares with horizontal blue lines on the trees that indicate the path is part of the Europawanderweg (European footpath) E10, which you'll follow all the way until Caputh. The forest road progresses for one kilometer before making a left turn in the woodlands and heading toward Teufelssee. Follow the sandy woodland trail upward toward Kleiner Ravensberg, the highest point on the route at 114 meters. From here you'll have a view across the entire forest landscape.

Following the E10 you'll arrive at the Waldhaus—an animal sanctuary featuring owls, raccoons, peacocks, and more—on the Großer Ravensburg hill. Take the path down to the left of the sanctuary, making a slight detour to the little forested lake of Teufelssee, before continuing on the E10, following the signposts directing you toward Caputh.

Walk along the moss-covered ground for 2 kilometers, cross over the train tracks and the Mochendorfter Chaussee, and follow the signposted forest path toward Caputh. After 1.5 kilometers on the Caputher

Heuweg, head right at the fork. After one kilometer, just as the woodland path leads into Caputh, follow the Am Waldrand path to the right between private gardens and woodlands all the way to Einstein's Summer House.

This two-storied wooden house served as a retreat for Einstein and his wife until they emigrated to the US in 1932. The restored home is open to the public on weekends; there's an entry fee of 5 euros, and tours are also available.

Carry on northward; you'll note that the painted blue square signs have been succeeded by blue dots. Walk northward on Templiner Straße for a kilometer, avoiding the swarms of cyclists that dominate this lakeside road. After 15 minutes, the entrance to the Forsthaus Templin will beckon you in from your woodland adventure.

FORSTHAUS TEMPLIN

With its wild and sprawling beer garden filled with goats, geese, and chickens, this woodland-house brewery is like a ranch for day-trippers. Built on an 18th-century estate near the shores of the Templinersee, it's the only brewery in Berlin and Brandenburg to make certified organic beers. Reflecting this, the restaurant and bar have a very rustic look and feel. In addition to its famed Stange, the brewery offers seasonal Bocks, Pilsners, Dunkels and Weizens, as well as homemade mustards, honeys, and schnapps. The menu is hearty and very German, featuring *Brotzeits*, fish dishes, and the occasional barbequed local sausage. Whatever your reason for visiting, you'll be sure to leave fulfilled.

ADDRESS

Braumanufaktur GmbH
Templiner Straße 102
14473 Potsdam
 +49 33 209217979
www.braumanufaktur.de

Photos © Yvonne Hartmann

WANDLITZSEE

A LAKESIDE FOREST RAMBLE

WANDLITZ, BRANDENBURG

▷⋯ STARTING POINT	⋯✕ DESTINATION
BAHNHOF WANDLITZSEE	**BRAUHAUS WANDLITZ**
🍺 BEER NAME	🀫 DIFFICULTY
WANDLITZER DUNKEL	**MODERATE**
🚆 TRANSPORT	🕒 DURATION
RB27 (HEIDEKRAUTBAHN)	**2.5 H**
⛰ ZONE	↦ LENGTH
C	**10 KM**
🔎 HIGHLIGHTS	〰 ELEVATION GAIN
STRANDBAD WANDLITZSEE, STOLTZENHAGEN SEE, DORFKIRCHE WANDLITZ	ASCENT: 50 M DESCENT: 40 M

DUNKLES

CLEAR DARK RUBY WITH
FOAMY HEAD

CARAMEL,
MALTY,
FLOWERS

SWEET CARAMEL
AND MALT

BITTERNESS

SWEETNESS

WANDLITZER DUNKEL. A wonderfully rich and extra-carbonated aromatic beer with a malty sweet-caramel profile and subtle undertones of flowers and citrus.

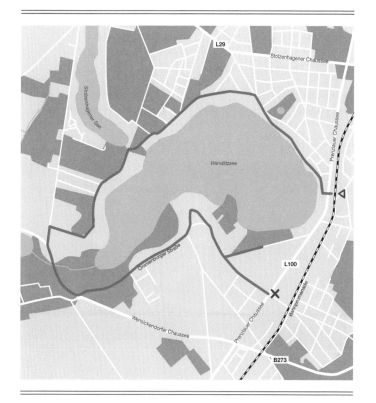

HIKE DESCRIPTION

The Wandlitzsee in Barnim National Park is one of the largest lakes in the region. Connected to the city by a single-track railway line, it's been a holiday destination for Berliners for over a hundred years. Throughout the summer, the magnificent and picturesque lake is filled with day-trippers bathing in its clear and calm waters. Private beaches with elegant piers are adjacent to grassy embankments and cobbled village roads. Along the lakeshore, regal estates are tucked away in the tranquil woodlands, radiating a stillness unique to such remote holiday villages.

The Heidekrautbahn, which once ran all the way up to Wilhelmsruh, is often filled with holidaymakers lugging beach gear and sports equipment. Alighting at the Wandlitzsee station, you'll immediately find yourself in the village center, facing the public beach.

Head directly toward the public beach and then walk counterclockwise around the lake, sticking to the shoreline. The path strays through woodlands and grassy embankments where you're free to stop and wade into the water. After a kilometer, the lakeside path joins Thälmannstraße. After 200 meters on Thälmannstraße, turn left on August-Bebel-Straße and follow it as it crosses a small brook and leads through a pine woodland. Soon you'll arrive at the lake's northernmost (and free) beach. Located opposite the region's other beautiful lake, Stolzenhagen See, the northern lakeside waterfront of Wandlitzsee provides great views, with windsurfers and stand-up paddlers doing their thing on the clear waters.

Follow the lakeside path for one kilometer until the end of Uferstraße. Take a right on Kirschallee and then turn left on onto Barsdorfer Straße and left again onto Oranienburger Chaussee. From there, turn onto Oranienburger Straße and follow it for a kilometer to reach the village of Wandlitz.

Enter the historical village square with its cobbled roads and old farm buildings on Kirchstraße, which winds around the 13th-century village church to reach the Barnim Nature Park Center, a museum dedicated to the history of the area. Head down Breitscheidstraße for 850 meters and arrive at Brauhaus Wandlitz. To return to Berlin, continue down Bernauer Chaussee (the continuation of Breitscheidstraße) to the Wandlitz train station.

BRAUHAUS WANDLITZ

The Gottfried family depicted on the brewery's logo have been a part of Wandlitz's hospitality history for over a century. The family opened the Rialto restaurant in 1992 and in 2013 decided to establish their own on-site brewery, which produces some of the finest beers in Brandenburg.

Located on the corner of Prenzlauer Chaussee and Bernauer Chaussee, the Rialto faces the family's beer garden, Zum Glück, on the other side of the road. At each of the two locations, a hearty selection of pub food is always available, along with freshly brewed beers straight from the tap. The standard Pilsners, Dunkels and Weizens are on offer all year round, with seasonal brews and specialties according to the time of year.

ADDRESS

Brauhaus Wandlitz
Prenzlauer Chaussee 123
16348 Wandlitz
+49 152 01733259
www.brauhaus-wandlitz.de

Photos © Daniel Cole

PANORAMAWEG

A SAUNTER THROUGH PRISTINE ORCHARDS AND FARMYARDS

WERDER, BRANDENBURG

▷··· STARTING POINT	···✗ DESTINATION
WERDER (HAVEL) STATION	**ZUM RITTMEISTER**
🍺 BEER NAME	DIFFICULTY
RITTMEISTERS SCHWARZBIER	**HARD**
🚆 TRANSPORT	⏱ DURATION
RE1	**4.5 H**
⛰ ZONE	↦ LENGTH
C	**15 KM (ONE WAY)**
👁 HIGHLIGHTS	〰 ELEVATION GAIN
TELEGRAPH MAST, GROSSER PLESSOWER SEE, PLESSOW	ASCENT: 100 M DESCENT: 100 M

5.0 % ALCOHOL CONTENT	SCHWARZBIER
👁	DARK CHESTNUT
👃	MALT, SMOKE, CHOCOLATE
👄	MALT, COFFEE, CHOCOLATE, NUTS

BITTERNESS | SWEETNESS

RITTMEISTERS SCHWARZBIER. With its roasted malt and nut aroma, this medium-sweet black-beer pleases with its subtle undertones of chocolate and coffee.

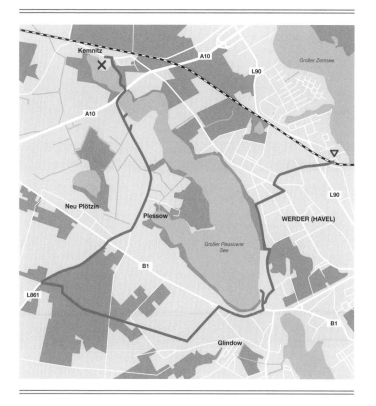

HIKE DESCRIPTION

A brief journey outside Potsdam and across the Havel River takes you to the small town of Werder, best known for its blossoms, fruit wines, and annual Baumblütenfest in May. Surrounding the town and its lakes are acres of farmland, with plum, cherry, apple, and other orchards that attract visitors from across the country. The area is also known for its homemade fruit wines, sold on almost every street corner and in all the restaurants, especially during the Baumblütenfest. In the midst of this wonderful landscape, a walk called the Panoramaweg meanders through the fields and up the Glindow Alps, offering views across the Großer Plessower See.

Leaving the station, head west across Phöbener Straße and up the hill on Kesselgrundstraße. After one kilometer, turn left on Kemnitzer Chaussee; then, after 250 meters, turn right on Gertraudenstraße. At the end of Gertraudenstraße, turn left on Am Plessower See and follow it for 2 kilometers. Just before you reach the junction with Berliner Straße, you'll come to a turnoff to Fischerhof Kühn, a lakeside smoked-fish restaurant that I highly recommend.

Turn right on Berliner Straße and follow it for 900 meters; then turn left on Glindower Gartenstraße, which is signposted as the Panoramaweg. Follow this country road uphill, past orchards and garden homes, for 800 meters; then follow the signposted route to the right until you reach a 19th-century telegraph mast overlooking the fields and water below.

Carry on through the fields of wheat and sunflowers and the orchards along the Panoramaweg for three kilometers. The country road you're on winds upward and curves in a clockwise direction, parallel to the lakeshore below. Depending on the time of year, you'll see different crops, farm animals, and flowering fruit trees, and maybe even the occasional fruit-wine salesperson.

When you hit Lehniner Chaussee, head east on it, leaving the Panoramaweg. At the bottom of the hill, after Werderaner Tannenhof, is a local farm shop where you can buy some of the fruit and fruit wines that the area specializes in.

Crossing Brandenburger Chaussee, the road turns into Plessower Hauptstraße and journeys into the charming old village of Plessow. Follow Plessower Hauptstraße for 1.5 kilometers, passing the old

village church and local farms as the road turns into a woodland path, which carries on for another 1.2 kilometers before arriving at a fork. At the fork, follow the path heading toward the right, which leads along the water's edge and then passes beneath the highway. Here, a small bridge will take you to the other side of the lake, where you'll head north, following the water's edge in a counterclockwise direction on the signposted E10 route. The route passes over a few secluded beaches and through some rich woodland before entering Rittmeister Park, where you'll see ample "Brauerei" signposts pointing you toward the end of your journey.

To get back from Zum Rittmeister, you can take a regular, direct bus to the train station (which doesn't run on Sundays) or follow the E10 along the water and back to your starting point.

ZUM RITTMEISTER

With its beautiful garden terrace overlooking the nearby lakeside, this idyllic and picturesque village restaurant and hotel is well worth a trip outside the city. Traditional and welcoming, the bar manages to walk the line between classy and pleasant with its chic interior and tranquil beer-garden setting. The exquisite food menu includes local and seasonal vegetables worked into traditional Brandenburg-Prussian dishes. The brewery serves up Pilsners and Schwarzbiers all year round, with additional offerings of fruit-flavored beers, including orange and apple varieties. The brewery also ventures into the world of spirits, which are of course also fruit flavored. At Zum Rittmeister, you can enjoy fine dining, relaxing afternoons beneath the chestnut trees, or an exceptional overnight stay.

ADDRESS

Zum Rittmeister Hotel und Catering GmbH
Seestraße 9
14542 Werder (Havel)-OT Kemnitz
+49 33 274646
info@zum-rittmeister.de
www.zum-rittmeister.de

Photos © Yvonne Hartmann

GRÜNHEIDE

DISCOVER BRANDENBURG'S SMALLEST BREWERY

GRÜNHEIDE, BRANDENBURG

▷··· STARTING POINT	···✕ DESTINATION
ERKNER S-BAHN STATION	**FLÜGEL'S HOF**
🍺 BEER NAME	🀱 DIFFICULTY
FLÜGELBRÄU DUNKEL	**MODERATE**
🚆 TRANSPORT	🕐 DURATION
S3	**2 H 40 MIN.**
⛰ ZONE	↦ LENGTH
C	**10.4 KM (ONE WAY)**
🔍 HIGHLIGHTS	〰 ELEVATION GAIN
HUBERTUSSTEG BRIDGE, WERLSEE LAKE	ASCENT: 50 M DESCENT: 50 M

5.3 % ALCOHOL CONTENT

DUNKLES

DARK BLACK

MALT, WHISKEY

WHISKEY, ROAST MALT, CARAMEL

BITTERNESS

SWEETNESS

5 4 3 2 1

5 4 3 2 1

FLÜGELBRÄU DUNKEL. A refreshing and well-balanced unfiltered dark beer with a strong roasted-malt flavor and notes of whiskey and flowers.

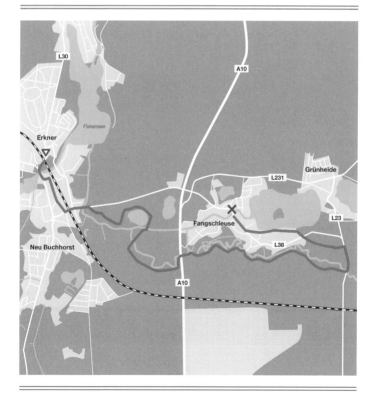

HIKE DESCRIPTION

Just outside Erkner, one of Berlin's neighboring towns, is an excellent woodland nature trail that passes through the Wupatz forest and along the Löcknitz, a small tributary of the Spree that flows through moorlands and wide-open meadows. The protected, sedate woodlands provide a breath of fresh air, and walkers here are few and far between. Not bad for a 20-minute train journey from Berlin!

Leaving the station, head west on Bahnhofstraße and then turn left on Friedrichstraße, heading straight through the town's busy center. At the end of Friedrichstraße, turn left on Fürstenwalder Straße and follow it for 600 meters.

After crossing the Löcknitz, take the small, well-signposted path leading into the woodlands on the south side of the road. Follow the path around the Wupatzsee and back across the Löcknitz. Continue following it to the right as it crosses the Hubertussteg bridge over the Alte Löcknitz, a small tributary of the Löcknitz. 150 meters after the bridge, turn left on the footpath and follow the blue markings until you reach a signposted junction. Take the footpath to the left going to Grünheide.

The footpath passes beneath the Froschbrücke, a little bridge decorated with oversized frog statues, and then through sheep-filled meadows. Carry on following the waterside path until you cross the road in front of the "Alte Liebe" house.

Continue following the waterside path until it reaches the main road, An der Löcknitz (about 2 kilometers). Turn left on An der Löcknitz and cross the Alte Löcknitz, keeping the German Wall Memorial to your right. After 300 meters, turn left onto a footpath just after the school grounds. Carry on into the woods on this footpath for 750 meters, cross Ernst-Thälmann-

Straße, and then turn left on Werlseestraße. After a few hundred meters, the clear waters of the Werlsee will come into view. At the end of Werlseestraße, turn right on Eichenallee and follow it until you reach Flügel's Hof, just before yet another bridge across the Löcknitz.

To get back to Berlin, there is a regular bus that runs from outside the café to the Erkner and Fangschleuse stations.

FLÜGEL'S HOF

With just a 50-liter brewing system and three fermentation tanks, the Flügel family established Brandenburg's smallest brewery in 2020. Located in the garage of the family's modest courtyard-café, the brewery serves unfiltered, flavorful brews made using only natural ingredients. The quaint and homely setup is a perfect pit stop for hikers in the area, offering indoor and outdoor seating and grilled foods, waffles, and ice cream. The café's homemade cakes are as appetizing as its beers and should not be passed up. The three taps serve up Helles and Dunkel beers throughout the year, with rotating seasonal brews.

ADDRESS

Flügel's Hof – Atelier, Brauerei, Café
An der Fangschleuse 3
15537 Grünheide (Mark)
+49 33 628857174
www.fluegels-hof.de

Photos © Yvonne Hartmann

ACKNOWLEDGEMENTS

This book would not have been possible without the help and support of Rich Carbonara, author of *Beer Hiking Bavaria*. His book provided the inspiration and catalyst for our work, and his walks throughout Bavaria have given us endless pleasure. It was Rich who connected us with and recommended us to Helvetiq, for which we will be forever grateful. If you're ever in Bavaria and looking for a guided tour, then reach out to him; you can depend on his bottomless tank of knowledge.

Another big shout-out to Joe Holler of *Beer Hike Nuremberg*, who has also been a great source of inspiration, knowledge, and all-round good-time vibes. Again, reach out to him for some very inspired beer experiences in Franken Bavaria.

A big thanks to all those who've joined us on our walks throughout Berlin and Brandenburg and kept us company. We raise our glasses to the people from all walks of life we've shared beers with along the way. And, of course, our deepest gratitude to Motas, for always leading the way.

Lots of gratitude to Marion Hartmann for proofreading and fact-checking; your attention to detail is impeccable. And to Lisa Khanna for allowing us to use her photography—the next round is on us.

To Hadi and Satu at Helvetiq: we salute you. Thanks for entrusting this work to us and pushing us to do more and better ourselves. You've opened a new door in the world of publishing, one that we've been searching for for so many years. We hope to collaborate with you for years to come.

A nod to The Craft Beer Channel for just being excellent and providing constant news and knowledge about the word of beer, and to Markus Raupach and Bastian Böttner for instigating written work on Berlin brewing just under ten years ago.

And of course, our biggest thanks and praise go to those who've helped futher and revolutionize the Berlin beer scene. We've lived in Berlin for many years and rekindling our love for the brew thanks to all the new breweries and taprooms that have found a home in the city has provided us with no end of pleasure. In particular, a nod to Hops & Barley for being such a fine and neighborly establishment, Protokoll Taproom for having such a great and varied selection, and Bräugier for just being awesome. May we all enjoy many more adventures and drinks in the years to come.

DO YOU KNOW OUR OTHER TITLES IN THE SAME SERIES?

**Beer Hiking
Bavaria**

978-2-940481-82-8

**Beer Hiking
New England**

978-3-907293-74-4

**Beer Hiking
Pacific Northwest**

978-3-907293-70-6

**Beer Hiking
Colorado**

978-1-94800-15-3

**Beer Hiking
Canadian
Rockies**

978-3-907293-89-8

**Whisky Walks
Scotland**

978-3-907293-66-9

AND MANY MORE...